The Piaf Legend

DAVID BRET

The Piaf Legend

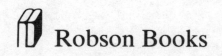 Robson Books

First published in Great Britain in 1988 by Robson Books Ltd,
Bolsover House, 5–6 Clipstone Street, London WIP 7EB.

Copyright © 1988 David Bret
British Library Cataloguing in Publication Data

Bret, David
　The Piaf legend.
　1.　popular music. Singing. Piaf Edith,
　1915–1963. Biographies
　I.　Title
　784.5'0092'4

ISBN 0 86051 527 3

Printed in Great Britain by
Biddles Ltd., Guildford and King's Lynn

A vous, Barbara, pour trente ans de chanson et pour nos jolis souvenirs de Pantin. 'La vie sans amis c'est comme un jardin sans fleurs.'

Contents

Acknowledgements

The author would like to thank the following for giving him permission to include extracts from the songs of Edith Piaf;

Chappell Music, 129 Park Street, London W1:
Les Mômes de la cloche [1936]; *De L'autre côté de la rue* [1943]; *'Hymne à l'amour* [1950]; *Mon légionnaire* [1937]; *Mon Dieu* [1960].

Southern Music Publishing Company, 8 Denmark Street, London WC2: *Paris Méditerranée* [1939]; *L'accordéoniste* [1940]; *Les trois cloches* [1946]; *Légende* [1956]; *La foule* [1957]; *Mon manége à moi* [1957]; *Les mots d'amour* [1960]; *T'es l'homme qu'il me faut* [1960]; *A quoi ca sert l'amour* [1962]; *Les gens* [1963]; *A L'enseigne de la fille sans coeur* [1952]; *Bravo pour le clown* [1953]; *Le gitan et la fille* [1958]; *Les flons-flons du bal* [1960]; *La belle histoire d'amour* [1960]; *Le fanion de la légion* [1937]; *Chanson bleue* [1949]; *La ville inconnue* [1959].

Noel Gay, London:
La vie en rose [1946].

Editions Salabert, Paris:
Milord [1959]; *Opinion publique* [1960].

Editions Paul Beuscher, Paris:
Où sont ils mes petits copains? [1940]; *C'est un monsieur très distingué* [1942]; *Tu es partout* [1941]; *C'etait une histoire d'amour* [1943]; *Mariage* [1947]; *Demain il fera jour* [1951]; *Les amants d'un jour* [1956]; *Et pourtant* [1958].

Editions Raoul Breton, Paris:
Monsieur Lenoble [1949]; *Je t'ai dans la peau* [1953].

Britico/S.D.R.M:
Une enfant [1952]; *Les neiges de Finlande* [1958]; *Je hais les dimanches* [1951].

Shapiro-Bernstein, London:
Non je ne regrette rien [1960].

Editions Intersong, Paris:
Roulez tambours [1962]; *Le droit d'aimer* [1962].

Editions Patricia, Paris:
J'en ai tant vu [1963]; *L'homme de Berlin* [1963].

The author would also like to express his appreciation to the following publishers for granting him permission to include extracts from various works in Britain, France and the United States:
Chivers Press, *The Autobiography of Edith Piaf*: The Wheel of Fortune.
Union Général d'Editions, *Ma vie* by Edith Piaf.
Grove Press Inc, *Manouche* by Roger Peyrefitte (published in France by Flammarion).
Editions Stock, *Edith* by Jean Noli.

Photographs for pages 1, 2, 3, 7 and 11A of illustrations supplied by the Keystone Collection; those for pages 4, 5, 6, 8, 9 and 11B by Camera Press, and those on pages 10 and 12 by Pictorial Press.

Introduction

There is little doubt that Edith Piaf was the greatest *chanteuse-réaliste* of this century. She was one of the world's foremost communicators, an authority on the human condition. Her life was like one of her songs: its beginning was humble and hesitant, its zenith colourful and lively, its end sad. Born in poverty in a squalid Parisian backstreet, Piaf quickly learned all about life's complexities, and these experiences were transferred to her songs in such a way that she was able to touch the hearts of millions. Her artistry and courage of conviction were profound, and for thirty years this tiny, black-clad woman battled continually against the sometimes insurmountable odds of hardship, heartbreak, near despair and, towards the end, illness and fatigue. For most of this time her beloved public shared her supreme triumphs and her worst tragedies.

Piaf's life was never lacking in her quintessential qualities of courage and love: courage to face the inevitable and love for her fellow men. Her ability to help those less fortunate than herself was mixed with a tireless desire to discover and launch a whole new generation of entertainers, many of whom would not have made it without her. Without these qualities, Piaf might have been termed 'just another singer'.

Piaf was unique in that she was able to transcend the conventional barriers imposed upon us by a foreign language. She never appeared in Britain yet she was, and still is, immensely popular on this side of the Channel. She refused to sing in Russia, yet when her death was announced the people of Moscow held a two-minute silence. Because her lyricists often wrote exclusively for her in Parisian argot, a dialect not unlike our own Cockney, it is often difficult to attempt more than a modest translation. Most of her songs are not transferrable, even from Piaf to any other French singer, and one can only offer inadequate paraphrases. Therefore the English adaptations of her works throughout this book are

11

not intended to be grammatically accurate, and serve only as a basis for those readers whose appreciation of Piaf's art is limited by language.

I never saw Piaf, but whilst researching this book her presence was more potent than ever, and my book is an attempt to thank her for the immense, heart-warming pleasure which she has given me over the last twenty-odd years. I have met many fascinating people, and have received little opposition.

I would particularly like to thank the singers Barbara and Dorothy Squires for their support when I felt like giving up. Also, I would like to thank the late Michel Emer, Christian Bourgois, Ralph Harvey, Jean-Christophe Averty, Marcel Blistène, Charles Aznavour, Pierre Desgraupes, Channel Four, the IBA and the BBC, Louis Dupont, Catherine Jan, Bernard Marchois of Les Amis d'Edith Piaf, the editors of the *Daily Express*, *Paris-Match* and the *New York Times*, and the many friends, colleagues and acquaintances of Edith Piaf who asked not to be named.

Most of all, from the bottom of my heart, I would like to thank Edith herself.

David Bret
July 1988

1

The Street

HER FATHER WAS Louis Alphonse Gassion, a travelling acrobat of no mean talent, and a rogue to boot who never refused any challenge to prove his virility. Gassion was a small man, just five feet tall, and weighing little more than six stone. He had been born in Falaise, Normandy, into a family steeped in show-business tradition; of his three sisters Mathilde and Zephoria performed on the tightrope until shortly before the Great War. Louise, with her husband and a friend, were internationally renowned as Krag's Trio, a troupe which successfully toured Britain, the United States and the Far East.

Edith Piaf's mother was Line Marsa, a street singer who by the time of her confinement had progressed to some of the better backstreet cafés and dives of Paris. In 1974 the author was in a bar on rue Montmartre drinking with an elderly couple who had actually heard her sing. Her voice, they claimed, was harsh and vibrant, yet with a strange heartfelt quality. Some years later the same couple had listened to Edith Gassion singing in exactly the same spot. The voices had been similar. Line Marsa's failure to hit the big time was due to bad luck, and not lack of talent. She had been born Annette Giovanna Maillard in Leghorn, Italy, in about 1898, and is known to have met Gassion at a Parisian fairground where she ran a roundabout and sold nougat. It mattered little that he was twice her age; Annette went to live with him at Sens, and they were apparently very happy until the summer of 1914 when Gassion was called up to fight.

Louis Gassion was as crafty as he was handsome. He knew the regulations that any soldier about to be married would be granted leave. The couple were married on 14 September 1914. Then Gassion returned to the front and the girl and

13

her mother (her father had died some time before) moved to Paris.

Of Louis Gassion's twenty or so children, the future Edith Piaf would be one of only a few to be born on the right side of the blanket. The birth itself is enshrouded in mystery, as with much of Piaf's early life. She herself liked to fantasise, although we have no reason to doubt her own account, told in *Au bal de la chance*, and in countless television and radio interviews, and in a serialisation of her life in *Paris-Match* a few years before her death. Annette, in labour, had sent her hopelessly confused husband out into the street to call an ambulance or to summon help from the nearby Hôpital Tenon. The hospital was on rue de la Chine, about fifteen minutes' walking distance from the Gassions' rooms at 72 rue de Belleville. For whatever reason, no help came, and two passing gendarmes, hearing the mother's groans, came to the rescue. The baby was born on a policeman's cape, spread out under the glare of a street-lamp, during the early hours of 19 December 1915.

Edith's birth certificate does state that she was born at 4 rue de la Chine, 20th arrondissement, but as this is the address of the hospital at which the mother had previously arranged to have the child, Edith's story is almost certainly the more accurate. In 1966 Maurice Chevalier unveiled a plaque over the doorway of 72 rue de Belleville:

> On the steps of this house was born the 19th December 1915 in the greatest destitution EDITH PIAF, whose voice, later, would overthrow the world.

The child was christened Edith, after the heroic English nurse Edith Cavell, who had been executed by the Germans only days before. For a second name her parents chose Giovanna, to remind the world that she had that much more of her mother in her. In fact, she loathed both the name and the woman who had brought her into the world.

Louis Gassion returned to the war. Line Marsa abandoned her daughter and went back to singing in the cafés. For a while Edith was left in the incapable hands of her maternal

grandmother, Mena Maillard; she was a thoroughly despic-
able character who lived in a hovel on the rue Rebeval.
Mena, hardly knowing one end of a baby from the other,
put red wine in the feeding bottle and left her unattended for
lengthy periods whilst she went out on the town. Needless
to say, the child fell ill. Louis Gassion came home on leave
at the end of 1917 to find her covered in scabs and crawling
with fleas.

Gassion took her to his mother's place in Bernay, Normandy. It was a cleaner, happier, healthier environment,
with just one snag. Number 7, rue Saint-Michel, where
Madame Gassion worked as resident cook, was a notorious
brothel.

The prostitutes adored Edith and she became their mascot.
For the next few years she, who had never known her real
mother, now knew several. The girls made her dolls. They
taught her how to play the piano; the establishment had
one of those lovely mechanical instruments which would
later turn up in many of Edith's most famous songs. One
immediately thinks of *Les amants d'un jour* and *Le vieux
piano*, which the lyricist Henri Contet must have written with
Bernay in mind:

> A piano is dead. She loved it when she was young, when
> she used to get drunk on its sadness and nostalgia. Now
> she drinks at the bar and sees imaginary hands on the
> keyboard, and kids in blue jeans talk about a washed-out
> bistrot and a has-been piano. But one day a soldier enters
> . . .

It astonished the girls, and their customers, that this tiny,
pretty child had such a natural ear for music. Even at the age
of three she could play one or two basic chords. And then,
quite suddenly, Edith developed conjunctivitis.

We do not know for certain whether or not she actually
went blind. Using whatever evidence there is, and this
again amounts to little more than the singer's personal
recollections, we must assume that she did. After all, she
had no reason to make up the story and this, added to
her lifelong faith in the saint who allegedly performed the

miracle which regained her her sight, should suffice to end the argument.

Grandmother Gassion was a sensible woman. She summoned a doctor, and Edith was examined. An inflammation of the cornea was diagnosed, and a cataract had developed. The treatment was horrendous: silver nitrate applied direct to the eyes. And when it failed the doctor merely declared that the child would remain blind for the rest of her life, which was just as well, he added, considering her surroundings.

The girls conferred amongst themselves, and formulated a plan. Money was not a problem: few brothels went bankrupt. The girls could have afforded a better, more learned physician. Instead, they closed the house for the day and took Edith on a pilgrimage to the shrine of Ste Thérèse, in Lisieux (although Ste Thérèse was not officially canonised until 1925).

Was it really a miracle? Had Grandmother Gassion secretly taken Edith to see another doctor? We shall never know. On 21 August 1921 Edith regained her sight, and from that day forth, Ste Thérèse, with her little shower of roses, played a vital role in the singer's life. She always wore her talisman about her neck. Once, when it had either been lost or stolen, she truly believed herself to be on the point of death and only recovered when a replacement was found. In later years, when sadly most of her better photographs depicted her in one hospital bed or another, Ste Thérèse's photograph or statuette was always on the bedside table, next to the Bible and the bottle of pills.

Of course, now that Edith could see, she had become aware of her surroundings. She saw pretty girls in expensive clothes, sailors and soldiers dropping in at all hours with flowers and gifts, only to leave after an hour or so. For the local priest, who had accepted her at the prestigious *Ecole Paul Bert*, the time had come to act. Summoning Louis Gassion, he gave him an ultimatum: if the child was not taken away from the brothel, she would have to be removed from the school.

Gassion whisked her away. Her show-business life had begun.

Father and daughter toured the provinces in a caravan, and with some degree of success. They even worked in Belgium. Theirs was a familiar act, made unfamiliar by Gassion's candid banter and by the urchin clinging to his heels like a ragged little dog. He would spread a tattered piece of carpet on the pavement, and the act would begin . . .

'Ladies and gentlemen! You are about to witness the finest *contorsioniste-antipodiste* in the business! My little daughter will make the collection. Afterwards, if you pay well, she will execute her perilous somersault!'

The child collected the money from the awestruck spectators. As for the somersault, it was never performed. Gassion saw to that, with a variety of excuses.

Les Gassions were popular, and made sufficient money to eat well and pay for their hotel room. Occasionally, if they stayed in any one town long enough, Edith would be sent to school, usually for the free handout of shoes and clothes. But if he was a loving, devoted father, Louis Gassion was also a harsh one. More than once Edith felt the back of his hand. He was a man of few scruples. Like Line Marsa, he was a heavy drinker. For the working classes in France during the period between the wars there was little else to do if one did not have a regular job. Gassion had a string of mistresses, few of whom could have enjoyed sharing a single room with an inquisitive child. As a result, Edith learned about sex at an early age, and later claimed that she had lost her virginity at fifteen. But Edith and her father were never what would be termed inseparable. They were simply close. When he died her tears were genuine; she never even attended her mother's funeral.

The magnificent singing career began one winter's day when Louis Gassion took ill, and had to be confined to his room. There was no money for food. Whatever they earned one day, they spent the next, and the rent for their squalid room was long overdue. The *concierge* had vowed that unless he coughed up, Gassion and his daughter would be thrown out into the street where they belonged.

How it happened is unclear. Whether her father ordered Edith to go out and sing in the street, or whether it was a natural reaction to do so, inherited from her wayward mother, matters little now. She was just ten years old, and her first song was *La Marseillaise*. When she returned to their room, her father was astonished. She had made more in an hour than they had earned together in a week!

At fifteen Edith left her father to make her own way in life. Ironically, the break came at about the same time as Gassion's involvement with Georgette L'Hôte, a young woman some seven years Edith's senior whom he had met after placing an advertisement in the personal column of a Nancy newspaper. Yeyette, as he affectionately called her, very soon fell in love with him and became pregnant. She, Gassion and Edith moved back to Paris where they rented a hotel room at 115 rue de Belleville. Georgette's baby was important so far as the post-1963 Piaf legend is concerned. She was Denise Gassion.

At about this time Edith met Simone Berteaut. Edith, who never called her friends by their full names unless displeased with them, nicknamed her Mômone. For some time they were inseparable. Mômone claimed to be Piaf's half-sister, but only after her death, and if in her famous book *Piaf* she implies that they were very close throughout the singer's life, this may well be true. Critics have observed that Mômone is not mentioned at all in either of Piaf's autobiographies, but this means nothing, for Marcel Cerdan is only mentioned briefly in *Au bal de la chance*, and he was definitely the greatest love of her life. Denise Gassion is also not referred to.

Edith and Mômone had a number of violent upheavals in later life, though they always apparently made up. Edith often referred to her as 'my demon spirit' or 'my evil genius'. Even so, they were together at every major step in Edith's life. Whether or not they were sisters, they were certainly friends.

With Mômone, Edith sang in the streets day and night. They stole food if they could not afford to buy it. Often they slept rough, in dank cellars or in cold, draughty buildings; and rarely alone. Theirs should have been a thoroughly deplorable way of life. In fact, for the first time in their lives they were gloriously happy because they were free to please themselves. They never realised, perhaps, that legally they were still minors, and that what they were doing was against the law.

Edith's first repertoire was both mature and macabre. Her songs included *Je suis vache* (I am a cow), *La fiancée du démon* (The devil's fiancée), and a very famous song immortalised by Damia:

> Dans ma névrose,
> J'ai pris des tas d'choses,
> Ether, morphine et coco,
> J'ai le cafard . . .
>
> (In my neurotic state,
> I took all kinds of things,
> Ether, morphine, cocaine,
> I've got the blues . . .)

Maryse Damia (1890–1978) known as *La Tragédienne de la Chanson*, was the greatest of all French popular singers before Piaf. She was the first of her genre to sing entirely in black, ordering a central spotlight to pick out only her face and hands. She sang successfully in Britain and had big hits with *Just a Gigolo*, *Johnny Palmer* and *Gloomy Sunday* (also a big hit in America for Billie Holiday). She did cover versions of several Piaf songs, and Edith even wrote a song for her in 1942.

Edith already knew the acrobat Camille Ribon (Alverne), and it was through his intervention that she began working in the army barracks with an enterprising young couple, Raymond and Rosalie. Together they formed the trio Zizi, Zozette and Zouzou. It was a brief but well-paid partnership, for soon afterwards Edith and Mômone were able to afford a room of their own in the Hôtel de l'Avenir, on rue Orfila.

Edith adored the army barracks and developed a lifelong passion for men in uniform: *légionnaires* in particular. There must have been many one-night stands, many unkept promises. The French Foreign Legion, the *Coloniales*, ordinary soldiers (these were the ones she loved the most) cropped up in her songs, off and on, for the next thirty years.

Her first serious love affair occurred early in 1932. His name was Louis Dupont, and he lived with his mother at Romainville, in the Seine–Saint-Denis area north-west of Paris. He was a fair-haired delivery boy who, possibly because of his stature (or more likely so as not to confuse him with her father), quickly became known as P'tit Louis. At nineteen he was three years Edith's senior, but much more gullible. It was love at first sight, and one wonders what this young man could have seen in Edith then, almost always dressed in rags or hand-me-downs, rarely clean, foul-mouthed and generally most unladylike. Yet almost immediately, Louis asked her to live with him.

Edith consented, though apparently neither she nor Mômone were prepared to move out of their hotel room. The three of them shared the tiny room and, it is said, the same bed, mindless of the scandal. In fact, the relationship between Louis and Mômone was not even platonic; they disliked each other.

Through Louis, Edith developed her passion for the cinema. She was particularly fond of American slapstick comedy. Charlot (Charlie Chaplin) was her favourite; years later they were to meet in Hollywood. But Edith's passion for the cinema was not a healthy one, or so her friends have often said. If she found a film that she liked, she would sit through it twenty, often thirty times, and whoever was with her had to put up with it. Often her friends would accompany her to the cinema in order to catch up on their sleep. Edith's life was hectic, and she kept most irregular hours, even then.

If Louis Dupont nurtured aspirations of a domesticated Edith, he had chosen the wrong girl. She was independent, and had ideas of her own. Moreover, she managed to get what she wanted. Confident that she would one day become famous, she continued to sing in the streets. Louis nagged her. He accused her of begging like a vagrant and found her a succession of jobs. Her first was at a factory, varnishing army boots. She loathed it, and hated being tied down. Because she was not Louis's wife, she opposed him in every way.

Soon she became pregnant. Now Louis *forbade* her to sing, and eventually she relented, agreeing that a pregnant girl standing on a street corner did indeed look like a vagrant. For a short time she worked in another factory, making wreaths. Mômone went with her.

The baby was born at the Hôpital Tenon in February 1933. She was christened Marcelle, and took her father's surname. The girls at the wreath factory clubbed together and bought the first layette. The baby wore it until it needed washing; then Edith burned it, and bought another. For the rest of her short life little Marcelle would wear only brand new clothes. Neither Edith nor her companion were interested in household chores, and Edith never would be.

Edith left the factory and returned to the streets, taking Marcelle with her by day, and leaving her with Louis at night. It was probably at this time that she met her celebrated but unnamed *légionnaire*. Sick and tired of her carping 'husband', she had already begun searching for a replacement. It was a pattern which would repeat itself constantly throughout her life. During the summer of 1933 she opened at the Juan-les-Pins, a seedy night-club on the rue Pigalle, then as now one of the most colourful and enticing districts of Paris. The Juan-les-Pins was run by a woman called Lulu, a huge 'butch' lesbian who always dressed in men's clothes. It would best be described as a gay bar, although it was also frequented by drug addicts, pimps, prostitutes, and many of the shadier characters from the Parisian underworld. P'tit Louis was furious. They had a violent quarrel, and Edith walked out on him, taking Marcelle and Mômone with her.

A new man entered her life – Albert, a muscular young pimp. Little is known of him, and again we have to rely on Edith's recollections. Certainly he must have been very handsome, or Edith would not have shown any interest in him in the first place. But if she loved him, she never had him entirely to herself. He had a girl working for him called Rosita, and there were others. Moreover, he was unkind, even brutal. When she refused to become a prostitute, Albert impounded a large proportion of the money she was earning by singing, and Edith allowed him to, willingly. He was the first of a long string of leeches who would bleed her dry, one way or another, taking advantage of her boundless generosity in order to line their own pockets. Surprisingly, Edith and Albert stayed together until one of Edith's friends, a girl called Nadia, drowned herself after being bludgeoned into prostitution by one of Albert's pimp friends. Only then did Edith leave him. Albert followed her, stalking her through the streets day and night. Luring her to his room, he pulled out a gun and shot at her. The bullet grazed her neck.

Edith's first major tragedy occurred in August 1935, whilst she was alternating between the Juan-les-Pins and Le Tourbillon, a nearby *bal-musette*. P'tit Louis arrived at her hotel room to inform her that their baby daughter had been taken to the Hôpital Tenon suffering from meningitis. Edith went there at once. The doctors had given Marcelle a lumbar puncture; the parents were told that her chances of survival were remote. Eight days later the child died.

Edith borrowed a nail-file from a friend and sawed off a lock of Marcelle's hair. Heartbroken, she returned to the Juan-les-Pins. Lulu organised a collection for the funeral. This stopped short of ten francs, and Edith did the one thing she had refused to do for Albert. She went on the beat.

According to Edith, as soon as she told her first 'customer' why she wanted the money, the man gave it to her and left. In spite of what has been recorded in subsequent biographies, there is no reason to doubt this.

The death of her daughter marked a significant turning-point in Edith's life. Her association with the Juan-les-Pins had lasted more than a year, during which time she had progressed no further than the four or five numbers of her opening night.

She decided that changes would have to be made, and set about searching for new horizons.

A third Louis entered her life – Louis Leplée.

2
Gerny's: *La Môme Piaf*

In pre-war Paris the opulence of the Etoile, that area taking in the Champs-Elysées, was a far cry from the squalor and misery of Belleville. Its clientele were infinitely richer, more choosy, and did not always take kindly to beggars.

Edith was no stranger to the area. She enjoyed a challenge; difficulties stimulated her, she claimed. She worked the Etoile with Mômone. Occasionally some carefree passer-by would drop a hefty tip into her cap, especially when prompted by Edith's stooge. Her big break came one afternoon in September 1935. Edith was leaning against the wall on the corner of the rue Troyon and the avenue Macmahon. She was singing *Les deux ménétriers*, yet another Damia song, when a well-dressed, elderly gentleman approached her. For a few minutes the man listened. After she had finished the song, he pointed out that by singing in such a manner, she would ruin her voice. An amused Edith, never short of an answer, coyly pointed out that she did not have a contract.

The man's attitude was genial. To Edith he was a toff because he wore gloves and carried a top hat and cane. All the same, she listened to his advice. He told her that his name was Louis Leplée, and that he was director of Gerny's, one of the city's most famous and exclusive cabarets, on the rue Pierre-Charron. Scribbling his name and address on a scrap of newspaper, and wrapping it in a banknote, he astonished her by concluding, 'Come and see me on Monday, at four o'clock, and I'll see what I can do!'

Leplée left, and Edith characteristically sang several more songs before moving to another patch. The money had impressed her, but she had vowed that success would never go to her head. Her upbringing had taught her never to believe in dreams. Dreams did not buy food.

She was one hour late for her appointment with Leplée, and this impressed him. 'One hour late is good,' he told her. 'What will you be like when you are a star?'

Louis Leplée was a homosexual with a penchant for dramatic female singers. Much as today, the great *chanteuses-réalistes* of 1935 commanded a huge gay following. Once, Leplée himself had been an entertainer, what would today be termed a drag-queen, when he had directed his own show at Liberty's, in the heart of Pigalle. The great showman, Polin, had been his uncle.

Leplée introduced her to his pianist, Jean Urémer. Then he asked Edith to go through her repertoire. This was extensive, although it consisted mostly of dramatic works made famous by Damia, Fréhel, and Yvonne George. Yvonne George came from Montparnasse and was highly neurotic, being both a drug-addict and an alcoholic. Fréhel, on the other hand, was a genius of song. Very fat and very crude, she would shock her audience into silence and perform highly emotive numbers such as *Adieu*. In spite of her success between the two wars she died in 1951 in abject poverty.

Leplée and Urémer were amazed. Edith's untrained voice was so pure that even its flaws were transformed into qualities. Leplée demanded her name. She told him: Edith Gassion. That, he said, sounded common. She told him her other pseudonyms: Tania . . . Denise Jay . . . and Huguette Hèlia, the name she had used at the Juan-les-Pins. None of these names suited Leplée.

He eyed her up and down. She was very small, less than five feet tall. She had scrubbed herself clean and put on her best, perhaps her only dress. Her hair was plastered down with soap into an untidy, unattractive fringe. Her mouth was smeared with crude red lipstick. From Leplée's point of view, she wore the unmistakable aura of the gutter. She was like a sparrow that had been left out in the cold; tired and bedraggled.

The French word for 'sparrow' is *moineau*, but there was already an entertainer called *La Môme Moineau*, a topless singer-dancer who had risen to fame during the early twenties. Leplée looked at Edith again, and had a brainwave. Here was a typical little guttersnipe, yet so sincere and incredibly charming, natural, and wholly convincing.

'The Parisian slang for *moineau* is *piaf*,' he told her. 'You will be called *La Môme Piaf*!'

A legend had been created.

Some reports suggest that Edith was singing *Comme un moineau* (like a sparrow) when Leplée first heard her, which would tie in well with this account and add to the legend. Edith herself, however, confirmed that it was *Les deux ménétriers*.

Leplée engaged her to open the Friday following. He told her to learn four songs for the occasion: *Les Mômes de la cloche, Nini peau d'chien, La valse brune*, and Lucienne Boyer's hit at the time, *Je me fais petite*. She was given a great deal of publicity too, despite the short notice. There must have been many show-business entrepreneurs, some of them Leplée's friends, who thought her mentor mad to risk his all with an unknown singer he had picked up, literally, in the gutter. And it *was* a risk. Leplée stood to become an immense success if his coup paid off; he would be the laughing-stock of Paris if it failed.

Edith panicked. She had nothing to wear for the première, and no money to buy a dress. However, a friend gave or loaned her money to buy needles and wool. She chose black, setting a precedent she was to follow throughout her career, and began knitting frantically. So another mania developed, this time for knitting. In later life, she would always attempt to knit a pullover for the current man in her life, and she would never finish the garment – which is what happened now. Friday came and Leplée discovered her locked in the lavatory at Gerny's, knitting like mad, with only minutes before her performance. Her dress still lacked a sleeve.

Furiously, she began unpicking the other sleeve. She would sing with bare arms, she declared, like her heroine, Damia. Leplée would not allow this. For one thing, her arms were too thin, and she would look like a scarecrow. And for another, there was only one Damia, as there would only ever be one Piaf . . .

The problem was solved by Yvonne Vallée, then the wife of Maurice Chevalier. Madame Vallée came into Edith's dressing room primarily to wish her luck. When she saw the dress with its missing sleeve, she loaned her her own beautiful silk scarf to drape over her shoulder. It was customary for *chanteuses-réalistes* to wear red scarves. This one was violet; from that night on, violet would be Edith's favourite colour.

Yvonne Vallée returned to the auditorium. Edith's nerves were raw. If Chevalier's wife was in the audience, then surely the great man himself would be there, too?

He was, sharing a table with Fernadel and the legendary Mistinguett!

Leplée introduced her personally. Many years later, when Edith gave her last gala performance from the top of the Eiffel Tower, she would be introduced by that eminent novelist, Joseph Kessel. Kessel was with Leplée back in October 1935. 'I was passing the rue Troyon the other day,' Leplée told the audience. 'I heard this young girl singing. Her voice overwhelmed me. Now, I would like you to listen to her. She is wearing no make-up, and her dress is the same one she was wearing when I first saw her. I give you . . . *La Môme Piaf*!'

Edith walked onto the stage and stood under the spotlight. There was an icy silence, and then the piano struck up the first bars of the opening song. Because she did not know what to do with her hands she planted them firmly on her hips. This stance became one of the Piaf trademarks. Nervously, she started to sing,

> C'est nous les mômes, les mômes de la cloche,
> Clochards qui s'en vont, sans un rond en poche!
> C'est nous les paumées, les purées d'paumées,
> Qui sommes aimées un soir, n'importe où!
>
> (We're the kids, the guttersnipes,
> Tramps who roam around, broke!
> Outcasts, clapped out outcasts,
> Loved for a night, no matter where!)

To begin with, the audience ignored her. This was the high society of Paris and if they had any problems of their own they preferred to leave them at home. They certainly did not want to listen to some vulgar little creature singing about her sorrows. And then it happened, during the second refrain! Edith took control. They set down their knives and forks and listened. By the third verse she had them right where she wanted them, in the palm of her tiny hand. The song ended and there was a glacial silence, worse than when she had first walked onto the stage. Leplée himself started the applause, and the auditorium exploded with shouts of 'bravo!' and 'encore!' Maurice Chevalier, it is said, stood up and yelled his compliments for all to hear.

La Môme Piaf had arrived!

The act had its share of drama, too. Yvonne Vallée's scarf had been held in place by a single pin, and Edith had been warned not to move her arms. Now, carried away by sheer emotion, she raised her arms. The scarf slithered to the floor, revealing her missing sleeve. No one laughed. Her first public was too enraptured. Here was a young girl, no more than a child, with the unleashed vocal force of a hurricane!

Admirers crowded into her dressing room, including the awesomely jealous Mistinguett, who befriended her, though she never really liked her and remained jealous of her success. Jean Mermoz, the world-famous aviator, bought her the entire basket of violets from the flower seller and invited her to sit at his table and drink champagne. She also met the poet, Jacques Bourgeat, and began what would become the strangest, most secret, relationship of her life . . .

To this day, little is known of what passed between the ageing poet and the little girl from Belleville. It was strictly platonic. Whenever Edith's tight schedule permitted, Bourgeat would take her to a small hotel in the peaceful Chevreuse Valley. There had been little or no education in Edith's childhood. Now, they read Gide together and listened to Chopin and Beethoven. Edith became an intellectual. During the next twenty-five years she would write her friend some two hundred letters. These highly confidential documents he bequeathed to the Bibliothèque Nationale; they will not be available to the public until the year 2004.

Despite the adulation, however, there were several humiliating incidents during her early days at Gerny's. Artistes of long standing were jealous of her success. Leplée had adopted her, practically, as his own daughter. She called him Papa. But most of the staff at Gerny's disliked her and thought her crude. And one evening she attended a dinner party given in her honour by the cabinet minister Jean de Rovera. In her own words 'they wanted to see this quaint little singer from Gerny's, this nine-day wonder who simply had to be seen before she returned to the gutter'. Rovera and his high-ranking friends used her as a butt for their jokes. She actually *did* drink out of the finger-bowl, though needless to say, she handled herself very well and gave as good as she got.

1935 drew to a close, and *La Môme Piaf* was still singing other artistes' songs. In those days singers had to visit music publishers in search of new material, little of which was ever forthcoming because it was invariably snapped up immediately by the great names of the day. New songs were expensive to launch, and few publishers took uncalculated risks. Edith did have several influential friends, though. One such was the writer, Raymond Asso.

Asso was secretary to Marie Dubas, one of the most popular entertainers in France at that time, and certainly Edith's favourite singer. Edith, Marie and Asso met for the first time, apparently, in October 1935, and Madame Dubas quickly became the young singer's *alter ego*. In those days Marie Dubas was one of the few artistes to carry around a tape recorder. She disliked making records (as much as Damia disliked microphones and therefore never used one at all during her long career) because she always maintained that live performances were the only true way of appreciating a performer. She only taped certain songs in order to monitor their response. Marie was so impressed with Edith that she invited her to sing in her dressing room, one afternoon after a matinée. Worn, unedited and incomplete, this tape of *La java en mineur* is the very first recording of the Piaf voice. The song was not heard by the public until Jean-Christophe Averty broadcast it in his programme, *Les cinglés du music-hall*

on France-Inter in June 1981, though Piaf recorded it fully
in 1937:

> Un doux refrain mélancolique,
> Dont la mélodie morde le cœur,
> C'est une java profond d'cœur!

> (A melancholy sweet refrain,
> Whose melody bites the heart,
> A heart-felt java!)

Soon after this meeting Edith went to the office of
the well-known publisher Maurice Decruck. Here another
singer, Annette Lajon, was rehearsing a new song. It was
called *L'étranger*, and was a poem by Robert Malleron,
set to music by a young, practically unknown composer,
Marguerite Monnot.

Edith listened to the song and was captivated. She
promised herself that by hook or by crook, she would sing it
at Gerny's that very night. She asked Decruck if he would let
her have the song, and when he declined she asked Annette
Lajon to sing it again . . . and again. Madame Lajon was
flattered. Little did she know that Edith was memorising the
song. Quietly, she slipped out of the office. She had a su-
perbly good memory and the song, give or take a few words
which she would work out herself, was firmly fixed in her
head. Juel, her accordionist at Gerny's, improvised on the
melody and the finished result was infinitely more pleasing
than the original. Leplée attempted to talk her out of singing
it, but sing it she did, and it brought the house down.

> J'ai rêvé de l'étranger,
> Et, le cœur tout dérangé
> Par les cigarettes,
> Par l'alcool et le cafard,
> Son souvenir chaque soir,
> M'a tourné la tête . . .

> (I dreamed of the stranger,
> And, my heart troubled

By cigarettes, alcohol and gloom,
Each night,
His memory sets my head reeling . . .)

A few evenings later, and quite by chance, Annette
Lajon heard Edith singing her song at Gerny's. Outraged,
she waited in the dressing room for the inevitable showdown.
Nothing happened; Edith apologised and the two women
became friends. Nowadays, Madame Lajon remembers
Edith with great affection, and although Edith will always
be associated with the song, it was Annette Lajon's version
of it which won her the *Grand Prix du Disque* in 1936. Edith
recorded the song on the eve of her twentieth birthday, cou-
pled with *Les Mômes de la cloche*. Cover versions followed
by Suzy Solidor, Damia and Marie Dubas, but none of them
quite matched up to the Piaf version. Even now, fifty years
on, its emotion is quite stunning.

Edith's first gala concert was at the Cirque Medrano on 17
February 1936. It was a charity show arranged to benefit the
widow of Antonet, the great clown and female impersonator
who had recently died. It is sufficient to say that she shared
the bill with Maurice Chevalier and Damia, amongst others.
During the first song, the microphone failed, but nobody
seemed to notice, least of all Jacques Canetti of Radio-Cité,
who immediately signed her up for a radio broadcast. This
went out on 15 March. *Reste*, a highly dramatic song by
Jacques Simonot, caused a sensation.

Maintenant que tout est bien fini,
Et que nos cœurs se sont repris,
Reste, que nous parlions un peu
Du temps ou nous étions heureux . . .

(Now that it's over,
And our hearts are recovered,
Stay, let us talk a little
Of the time when we were happy . . .)

After the broadcast the Radio-Cité switchboard was
swamped by listeners begging to hear more of *La Môme*

Piaf, in those days unusual. Jacques Canetti, who was also producing her records, subsequently signed her up for more broadcasts. She sang on Radio-Cité for ten weeks!

On 6 April 1936 tragedy struck for the second time.

Edith had been out celebrating with friends. Remembering how Papa Leplée always chided her for staying out late, she telephoned his apartment at 83 avenue de la Grande Armée to let him know that she was all right. Someone else took the call, and ordered her to return at once. A very baffled Edith arrived at the apartment to be greeted by a horde of onlookers, press reporters and police. Louis Leplée had been murdered.

Imagine the poor girl's distress as her world came crashing about her ears. And worse was to follow. The subsequent police investigations were made public; the actual interrogation of *La Môme Piaf* was captured for posterity on newsreel film and shown in every cinema in Paris. For Edith, the scandal was horrendous.

The crime was never solved. Shortly before his death Leplée had concluded a business deal and it is known that he had taken a large amount of money back to his apartment. He had boasted of this the night before at Gerny's. On the morning of 6 April four young men had barged into his apartment. After gagging the maid, they had entered Leplée's bedroom, demanding money which in all probability he owed them. There had been a scuffle. Leplée had panicked and a single shot had been fired. The bullet had entered his brain below the left eye, killing him instantly.

No doubt Edith would have known the killers. Many of her friends were shady characters from the Parisian underworld she had come to know whilst working at the Juan-les-Pins. Leplée had made no secret of his sexual preferences; according to his housekeeper he had entertained handsome young men at all hours. It is even possible that one of his killers was a bisexual lover shared by Edith and Leplée, though of course Edith, who always thought her men had eyes for her alone, would have been unaware of this.

The enquiry was clumsily handled by a Commissaire Guillaume, a far from gentle man who was used to dealing with thugs and whores. He put Edith through hell. Whilst he was aware that she had not pulled the trigger, he was sure that she knew who had. Though not a prostitute, she was protected by pimps, and Commissaire Guillaume hoped that one of these would come forward with vital information. He never did, and Edith was eventually allowed to go free.

One by one her friends deserted her. No one wanted to be associated with a possible murderess, and soon only a handful of close friends remained: Robert Juel, her accordionist; Jacques Bourgeat and Jacques Canetti; and Germaine Gilbert, one of the singers from Gerny's, which was now closed down. Most important of all there was Marguerite Monnot, who would become her best friend and composer of some of her most celebrated songs.

Publicly, she was defended by a young journalist. Marcel Montarron wrote for a weekly publication, *Le Détective*, which had been established in 1927. For the issue dated 16 April 1936 he did a double-page spread on Edith. Her photograph, taken at Leplée's funeral and showing her weeping on the arm of a friend, bore the caption,

THE FOUR KILLERS
Disowned by his comrades of vice, Louis Leplée had only women, *La Môme Piaf*, and Laure Jarny to weep at his funeral.

In his article Montarron scathingly attacked those sensationalist publications which had suddenly capitalised on the Leplée affair by serialising, in comic-strip fashion, various episodes of Edith's 'pathetic, scandalous life'.

At Leplée's funeral one of Edith's former colleagues from Gerny's told her, 'Now your protector's dead, with your talent it won't be long before you're back on the streets.'

How wrong she would be!

3

Edith Piaf: Birth of a Legend

Any other singer might have given up. Not Edith. More determined than ever, she picked up the threads of her career and began looking for work. She was offered a contract with Odett's, a somewhat disreputable night-club in the heart of Pigalle's red light district. Here she discovered the true meaning of hostility. The public did not wish to listen to *La Môme Piaf*; they wanted to gloat over the girl who had been a central character in the Leplée affair. One night, Edith recollects, someone whistled (a sign of derision in France). Needless to say, when her contract with Odett's expired, she did not renew it, even when offered more money.

Her immensely successful radio series ended, and Jacques Canetti sent her on a tour of the local cinemas, performing several songs in between main features. It was common practice; even the famous Bluebell Girls worked the cinemas initially. Though not always popular with her audiences, she was nevertheless working and gaining essential experience. She met an impresario, Fernand Lumbroso, then working for Marian Oswald, the darling of the intellectual set during the 1930s. Lumbroso booked her on a tour of the provinces. Again, she was working the flea-pit cinemas, though with a bad reputation, who was she to refuse them? The first cinema was in Brest, ideal for Edith and her companion Mômone, because the port was teeming with sailors who flocked to see her. They made so much noise during her performances, and caused so much trouble outside the stage door, that the cinema manager complained to Lumbroso. Edith was summoned back to Paris, given a severe ticking-off, and promptly packed off to a series of engagements in Belgium.

When she eventually returned to Paris, she had a brief love affair with the singer-songwriter Roméo Carlès. They met at Le Globe on the boulevard Strasbourg, an artistes' hang-out and intellectuals' rendezvous. Their association lasted but a few months, and little is known of it other than the fact that Carlès gave her two fine songs: *Simple comme bonjour* and *La petite boutique*.

> Je sais dans un quartier désert
> Un coin qui donne des airs
> De promesses aristocratiques.
> J'y découvris l'autre saison,
> Encrassée entre deux maisons
> Une minuscule boutique . . .
>
> (I know a corner in a deserted quarter,
> Which offers airs
> And aristocratic promises.
> I discovered there, a while ago,
> A tiny shop,
> Squeezed between two houses . . .)

For Edith, however, things were slowly going from bad to worse. In desperation, she fled to Raymond Asso and begged him to look after her. Asso seized the opportunity, and his initial response was to offer her a song that he had just written, *Mon légionnaire*. Edith turned it down. Asso offered it to his boss, Marie Dubas, and she recorded it. Edith was furious. Asso consoled her by securing her a contract at the Boîte à Vitesse in Nice, a tiny cabaret in the basement at Maxim's. Edith arrived in Nice filled with enthusiasm only to discover to her horror that the Leplée affair had followed her. Slogans appeared on billboards next to her name: DID *LA MÔME PIAF* MURDER LOUIS LEPLÉE? COME AND SEE FOR YOURSELVES!

At first Edith considered returning to Paris. Then she decided to make the adverse publicity work for her, and the gamble paid off handsomely. Her first performance attracted newspaper reporters and other scandal-mongers. Then, when her audiences realised that she could *sing*, the people came to see her in droves, time and time again. Her accompanist was René Cloërec, who composed the music for several of her early songs, including the spoken *C'est toi le plus fort* which she sang for many years and recorded more than once, and *Paris-Mediterranée*. This latter song was actually inspired by Edith's train journey from Paris to Nice, and the words were supplied by Raymond Asso.

On the train I was sitting next to a handsome young man in the third-class compartment. Throughout our journey we smiled at each other. Then he held my hand and I slept with my head on his shoulder. At Marseilles two police officers were waiting for him. They handcuffed him and led him away and . . .

Le soleil rédoublait ma peine,
Et faisait miroiter ses chaînes.
C'était peut-être un assassin!

(The sunshine doubled my pain
And made his shackles shimmer.
Perhaps he was a murderer!)

At the Boîte à Vitesse Edith played to capacity audiences for a month, and the management signed her up for a further eight weeks. In Nice, on 19 December 1936 she celebrated her twenty-first birthday. Then she returned to Paris, and more problems.

Raymond Asso had promised to look after her, but it was not as easy as that. He was living with a woman, Madeleine, in Pigalle's Hotel Piccadilly. Moreover, wherever Edith went, Mômone was sure to be close behind, shadowing her and tending to get on everyone's nerves. Between them, Edith and Asso resolved the situation. No one quite knows how it happened, but Madeleine left, and Mômone got married. Edith and her flamboyant-looking songwriter moved into the Hotel Alsina on the avenue Junot.

Here, Asso set about remoulding her. He became her Svengali, and theirs was a very strange affair indeed. Asso later said that she looked like a Spanish beggar. She called him Cyrano, on account of his prominent nose. But the sheer combination of their talents resulted in a change in the entire world of the *chanson*, practically overnight. Asso and Piaf needed each other. The one would have been nothing without the other.

Asso was not a gentle, persuasive man as Leplée had been. Edith was a handful. She had to be bawled and bludgeoned into shape. Their relationship began and ended badly. Asso was possessive; he wanted Edith to stay with him and sing only his songs. She reciprocated by cheating on him with other men. She never forgave him for offering *Mon légionnaire* to Marie Dubas. Asso had made up for the error by writing her another song, *Mon amant de la coloniale*, but this in turn had been covered by a now-forgotten *chanteuse* called Andrée Turcy. Incredibly, Edith and Asso stayed together for three years. This was not because she loved him, but because there was a severe shortage of songwriters of his calibre. As soon as she found one, she deserted him. It practically put an end to his career. After Piaf, Asso wrote few successful songs.

Through Asso, Edith met the Bretons. They were the most respected music publishers of their day, and were affectionately known as *le Marquis* and *la Marquise*. Raoul Breton had discovered and launched Charles Trenet, and other artistes to pass through their doors were Fréhel, Barbara, and Les Compagnons de la Chanson.

The Bretons now set about moulding *La Môme Piaf*. It must have been an invidious task. She was introduced to Parisian society. She was whisked off to the couturiers, which evidently suited her because she adored dressing up and had a passion for hats, collecting them all her life and hardly ever wearing one. But she did not take kindly to the beauticians' advice, and she flatly refused to take singing or elocution lessons.

She told the Bretons, 'The only lessons I'm interested in are hearing Marie Dubas sing!'

Edith never imitated Marie Dubas. She never imitated anyone. The great Damia, in a radio interview with Jacques Chancel on the eve of her eightieth birthday in 1969 accused Edith of copying her style. This was a grossly unfair claim coming from a usually genial woman. However, Edith did learn from both Marie Dubas and Damia how to handle an audience and develop a sense of propriety when arranging the order of her programme.

Asso took her to see Marie Dubas at the ABC, then the most prestigious music-hall in Paris. To her horror, her heroine sang *Mon légionnaire*. Edith is reputed to have hit Asso. Not to be outdone, she recorded the song on 28 January 1937, snubbing Asso, Marie Dubas, Damia, and all the other artistes who had interpreted *Mon légionnaire*. She re-recorded it a year later, and it would remain one of her best-selling records. She claimed that she had a divine right to sing the song because it was based on one of her own experiences.

> J'sais pas son nom,
> Je n'sais rien d'lui,
> Il m'a aimée toute la nuit,
> Mon légionnaire.
> Il était mince, il était beau,
> On l'a mis sous le sable chaud,
> Mon légionnaire!
>
> (I don't know his name,
> Or anything about him,
> He loved me all night long,
> My légionnaire!
> He was slim and handsome,
> They buried him under the hot sand,
> My légionnaire!)

The ABC was run by Mitty Goldin, a stubborn Hungarian *émigré* not renowned for offering exorbitant fees. Asso wanted his young protégée to sing at the ABC at whatever cost. He went to see the impresario, and was promptly shown the door. Though Edith's records were selling well, Goldin declared that no singer with her reputation would ever set foot on his stage.

For many weeks Asso persisted, making a general nuisance of himself. Mitty Goldin gave in and offered Edith a spot in the first half of the programme. Meanwhile, she appeared in a gala for the Popular Front at the Vélodrome d'Hiver. It was almost a repeat performance of her first gala at the Cirque Medrano; the microphone failed and she completed her act without it – and still managed to shake the hall on its foundations.

Edith worked the ABC from 26 March to 15 April 1937. She was no longer *La Môme Piaf*, but Edith Piaf. Goldin had insisted on the change. During rehearsals she had worn a simple black dress with pockets and a white lace collar. On the evening of the première she removed the collar because she thought it interfered with the spotlight on her face. She kept the pockets; she still did not know what to do with her hands. The little black dress became her trademark.

Each performance was a sell-out. No one was interested in the star of the show, only in this tiny girl with the all-powerful voice and genuine, heartfelt sincerity. Her greatest success was *Le fanion de la Légion*, which Asso, the ex-légionnaire, had written especially for the opening night.

> Ah! Là-Là-Là, la belle histoire,
> Y a trente gars dans le bastion,
> Torse nu, rêvant de bagarres,
> Et dans le vent claque un fanion
> C'est le fanion de la Légion!
>
> (What a fine story!
> Thirty boys in the bastion,
> Bare-chested and dreaming of brawls
> And the flag clattering in the wind,
> The flag of the legion!)

The music for the two Legion songs had been composed by Marguerite Monnot, now a close friend and affectionately known as Guite. As a child Guite had played Mozart in the Salle des Agricultures. She had later studied under Nadia Boulanger and the great concert pianist Alfred Cortot. Her first professional work had been *Ah, les jolis mots d'amour*, hummed in a French film by Alice Tissot and Claude Dauphin, but it was her association with Piaf which really brought her fame. On the other hand had it not been for Marguerite

Monnot, Edith's rise to fame might not have been quite so meteoric. Piaf and Asso. Piaf and Monnot. Monnot and Asso. They all made each other.

After the ABC performance Edith was offered a small part in a now-vanished film, *La garçonne*, directed by Jean de Limur and featuring Marie Bell. In it she sang *Quand même*, by Louis Poterat, a man who would feature strongly in her career towards the end of her life.

Between 29 May and 4 June 1938 she participated in *Le Spectacle de la Jeune Chanson Française* at the Bobino, and for this Asso and Max d'Yresne came up with *Madeleine qu'avait du cœur*, a remarkably mature song for its time, and almost certainly directed at the woman whom Asso had ousted in order to retain Edith's affections.

On 28 October she returned to the Bobino in her own show, with a programme of songs written almost exclusively by Monnot and Asso, One, *Je n'en connais pas la fin* became immortal not only in French but later in English.

> Depuis quelque temps l'on fredonne
> Dans mon quartier une chanson,
> La musique en est monotone
> Et les parôles sans façon.
> Ce n'est qu'une chanson des rues
> Dont on ne connaît pas l'auteur
> Depuis que je l'ai entendue
> Elle chante et danse en mon cœur!
>
> (This song's been going around my neighbourhood
> Monotonous music, meaningless words,
> It's only a street song,
> I don't know who wrote it,
> But since I heard it,
> It sings and dances in my heart!)

On 11 November Edith appeared in a gala at the ABC, sharing top billing with Marie Dubas. By now, her affair with Asso had begun to wilt. When he was called up on 4 August 1939 a replacement had already been found.

She was singing at Le Night-Club, on the rue Arsène-Houssaye. Before her performance, which always began late, she would drop in at the nearby Caravelle Bar for a drink with friends. It was here, one night, that she met Paul Meurisse, a budding young singer who had recently been engaged by L'Amiral, a nearby cabaret. Meurisse was twenty-six, good-looking, with sleeked-down dark hair and alluring eyes. In *Ma vie* Edith recollects that he sang badly. He was very snobbish, in direct contrast to the rashly outspoken little singer, and he was the very first of her men to treat her like the lady she had never been, helping her on and off with her coat, opening the door for her, holding her chair whilst she sat down.

It was love at first sight. One evening Meurisse invited her to a party at his home; she stayed with him for two years. Their affair was rather more tumultuous than Edith's previous one. It was well publicised, too. Edith smashed all the crockery; she wrecked his valuable wireless, accusing him of showing more interest in it than in her; she cursed and swore at him in public, and embarrassed him by asking her friends around for the night, Mômone in particular. One interesting anecdote concerns the singer, Tino Rossi. Edith and Meurisse had had a row, and she had walked out on him and gone out with Tino. Over dinner, she poured out her feelings for the hapless Meurisse, so much so that Tino telephoned his friend, hoping to get them to make up. As soon as Meurisse arrived Edith flew at him and attacked him with a champagne bottle – fortunately without injuring him. Leaving the restaurant, he waited for her out in the street. The ensuing scene, with the taxi driver waiting to take them home, must have been hard for a man of Meurisse's breeding to swallow. Edith kicked and swore; he slapped her and dragged her into the taxi, unaware that the incident had marked the beginning of his downfall.

It appalled Meurisse that Edith could live in a shabby hotel like the Alsina, even if she did have a secretary by now, and a Chinese cook. Mômone reappeared on the scene, asking for hand-outs now that her husband had gone off to fight. Her presence nauseated Meurisse. He rented an apartment on the fashionable rue Anatole-de-la-Forge, close to the

Etoile; Edith moved in with him. It was her first apartment. But before the transfer there was to be one final, ugly scene with Asso, who ironically had come home on leave. For the rest of his life Asso felt bitter towards her, and there was only one more song from him. In 1952 she recorded his poem, *Mon ami m'a donné*.

Living close to the Etoile suited Edith. She still had the secretary and Tchang, the cook. However, with Meurisse she had moved well up the social scale, which did not suit her. Her Belleville upbringing was part of her special magic, on and off the stage, and for the rest of her life she would turn her nose up at what she called *l'honorable société*. There was one exception during her relationship with Meurisse.

His name was Jean Cocteau.

Edith had met this enigmatic man at the Bretons' house. At once he had baptised her 'the poet of the streets'. He lived at the Palais Royal on the rue de Beaujolais. His house had a private cellar-club, one of the first in Paris before the St Germain-des-Prés era. Here he entertained his friends. Edith went there regularly, mixing with and making friends with such distinguished personalities as Madeleine Robinson, Yvonne de Bray, and Cocteau's lover, Jean Marais. She became the *coqueluche*, the darling of the intellectuals. Yvonne de Bray, it is said, shared Edith's passion for drinking, and it was during one particularly heavy session that Edith opened her heart about her feelings towards Meurisse. She told Yvonne about their brawls and how she threw things at him or smashed the plates against the walls before storming out and getting blind drunk. She also told how Meurisse exacted his revenge; he would treat her with total indifference, lounging on his bed in his fancy silk dressing-gown, pretending to read the newspaper, fully aware that he was the most boring man she had ever met, yet knowing all the same that she could not live without him.

Yvonne de Bray repeated the story to Cocteau, and this is how the play *Le bel indifférent* came to be written. Cocteau wrote it especially for Edith, and not for Suzy Solidor, as has been suggested.

At first, Edith was reluctant to accept the part. She had never thought of herself as an actress, and certainly did not see herself in the Robinson-de Bray mould. Persuaded by Cocteau and his entourage, she agreed. The play opened in the spring of 1940 at the Bouffes Parisiens, sharing the bill with *Les monstres sacrés*, another Cocteau masterpiece staring Yvonne de Bray and Madeleine Robinson.

The plot was relatively straightforward and Edith was given all the dialogue, and had to hold the stage for thirty minutes. Meurisse, who would never make it as a singer because Edith had called him tone-deaf, had taken up playing minor roles in the theatre. But if he was expecting a lot out of Cocteau's play, he was to be disappointed. On stage, he did not have to utter a single word!

The scene is a tawdry hotel room, illuminated by a street-lamp outside the window. As the curtain rises the woman is alone, pacing up and down, waiting for Emile, her lover, to come home. He enters, puts on his dressing-gown, lights a cigarette, and lounges on the bed reading his newspaper. The woman addresses him, but he ignores her. Her moods then change by the minute: passion, hatred, love, spite. She throws fits and curses him. She humbles herself, she weeps. Emile falls asleep, and she wakes him. He gets up and starts to dress; she watches him, knowing only too well that he is going to spend the night with his mistress. At first she threatens to kill him; then she implores him to stay. Unable to stand any more he slaps her. Finally, he walks out. She runs across to the window and calls out to him as the curtain falls.

Le bel indifférent was a resounding success. Some years later, when interviewed for BBC Television's celebrated film-biography *I Regret Nothing*, Meurisse said that though Piaf was a bad actress, she acted well in the play much as General de Gaulle, a very bad singer, had sung *La Marseillaise* exceedingly well. Hardly a compliment, though the reviews for the play speak for themselves. Edith even offered an encore one night when Madeleine Robinson was taken ill; she took over Madeleine's role in *Les monstres sacrés*! Meurisse, however, did not complete the run; he received his call-up papers. Edith actually wrote to the Minister of War, and won a ten-day reprieve whilst a replacement was found for the role of Emile. She settled on a young actor called Jean Marconi.

During the run of the play Edith took a night off and on 9 May 1940 she appeared at the Bobino in a gala concert for the Red Cross. Sharing the bill with her were Maurice Chevalier, Johnny Hess, and Marie Dubas. This was one of the rare occasions when she was unfaithful to her little black dress; she wore an air-force blue suit because there were hundreds of RAF boys in the audience. Her closing song, for which she had written the words and Marguerite Monnot the music, caused a near-riot. It was called *Où sont-ils mes petits copains*? During the last verse the spotlight on her face gradually opened out until the entire stage had become flooded with the red, white and blue of the French tricolour. The audience rose to its feet and sang with her,

> Où sont-ils tous mes copains
> Qui sont partis un matin faire la guerre?
> Où est-il, mon beau p'tit gars
> Qui chantait, 'On r'viendra,
> Faut pas s'en faire?'

> (Where are all my mates
> Who left one morning for the war?
> Where is my handsome lad
> Who sang, 'We'll be back,
> There's nothing doing?')

Paris was at war. Raymond Asso had already been called up. Meurisse failed his army medical – he probably had bronchitis, from which he would suffer on and off for the rest of his life. He came home to discover that Mômone had temporarily moved into the apartment. This time there was a reason – her husband had been killed fighting.

Le bel indifférent closed at the Bouffes Parisiens, but Edith joined up with Meurisse in Toulouse, beginning a lengthy tour of the unoccupied zone. There was even talk of another play now that Cocteau too had travelled south. He had adapted his own story, *Le fantôme de Marseille*, with Edith in mind. It told a sorrowful tale: and old man meets and falls in love with a girl, who is actually a boy in disguise on the run from the police. Edith never gave her reasons for turning the play down – at least not publicly. Perhaps she thought at the time that one play had been enough, that she would be neglecting her vocation as a singer. Perhaps she intended appearing in the play after the war, when Cocteau returned to Paris – if so, her future commitments prevented this. We may never know.

4

Star without Light

During the war years Edith Piaf became one of the unsung heroines of occupied France. Whilst some of her contemporaries opted out by moving south, and one or two even collaborated with the Germans – who could forget the pathetic piece of newsreel with an equally pathetic Maurice Chevalier trying to excuse himself? – Edith's nerve, courage, and love of her countrymen knew no bounds. She finished touring with *Le bel indifférent*, and returned to Paris. She had to report regularly to the *Propagandastaffel* on the Champs-Elysées in order for her songs to be vetted before she could perform; to have refused would have resulted in a total ban. She fared well under the Germans because she always stood up to them; some of her fellow artistes were not so lucky. Arletty had her head shaved. Marie Dubas, a Jew, spent two years in South America and finished off the war in Portugal. Michel Emer and Marcel Blistène (of whom more later) were forced into exile in the unoccupied zone.

Edith hated the Germans and all that they stood for, yet she was sensibly circumspect towards their commandants in order to achieve her heart's desire: to sing for French prisoners-of-war in the concentration camps. Caring little for personal danger, she became *marraine de guerre*, literally 'godmother of war', to the prisoners of Stalag III in Germany.

She had met a young woman called Andrée Bigard early in 1940. They had become close friends, so close that Edith had appointed her her secretary, a job which amounted to little more than opening mail, answering the telephone and collecting press-cuttings. Although rarely short of a man, Edith always needed a woman close at hand to confide in. Mômone was always turning up, of course, and Edith's 'demon spirit' was all the more in evidence between lovers,

45

or when there was no man around. At this time, however, even Mômone was otherwise occupied, and as Marguerite Monnot was busy elsewhere, Andrée Bigard filled the gap.

Edith was horrified at some of the things she saw in Stalag III. She recognised some of her old friends from Belleville-Menilmontant. Andrée Bigard accompanied her as part of her entourage, and as soon as Edith discovered that her friend was working secretly for the Resistance, the two women formulated a plan. The Germans were as fond of Edith's singing as the French – they still are – and even though her lyrics had been closely scrutinised by the authorities, this did not prevent her from flinging Hitler in their faces whenever she could, and with an audacity second to none. One of her songs, *Il n'est pas distingué*, had been first introduced by Fréhel in the early thirties. Edith had recorded it in May 1936 and it had appeared on the flipside of *Les deux ménétriers*. The recording producer Pierre Hiegel broadcast it by mistake during one of his radio shows in 1940 and was severely reprimanded for doing so. This did not prevent Edith from singing it to the prisoners, in Bellevilloise *argot*, so that only they understood what she was singing about.

> Hitler est sur le tapis!
> Moi, Hitler je l'ai dans l'blair
> Et j'peux pas l'renifler
> Les Nazis ont l'air d'oublier
> Que c'est nous dans la bagarre
> Qu'on les a dérouillés!

> Hitler's on the mat!
> I've got him by the brush
> And I can't snivel at him!
> The Nazis tend to forget
> That we knocked the rust off them
> In the brawl!

And not only that! Edith often expressed her humble gratitude towards the camp commandant for his hospitality by asking his permission to sing the Hitler anthem. Naturally, this was always granted, though Edith had adapted it slightly by supplying her own colourful French lyrics. The anthem became *Dans le Cul*.

> Dans le cul, dans le cul!
> Nous aurons la victoire!
> Ils ont perdu toute espérance de gloire,
> Ils sont foutus,
> Et le monde en allégresse!

> (Up your arse, up your arse!
> Victory will be ours!
> They've lost all hope of glory,
> They're fucked up,
> And the world rejoices!)

One can imagine the explosive atmosphere amongst the prisoners with all the German soldiers standing to attention, and Edith, straight-faced and singing her heart out!

After each performance Edith and Andrée Bigard mingled with the prisoners, chatting to them and memorising their names and addresses. Edith then asked permission to have her photograph taken with everyone, prisoners and officers alike. The photographs, she declared, would be used for publicity back in Paris to show the people how well they were being 'looked after' by their captors. Her request was never refused.

The films were taken back to Paris, where Andrée Bigard had them developed and enlarged. Whenever possible the heads and shoulders of the prisoners were cut off and pasted onto false identity papers.

Later, the papers were smuggled back into the camp – Edith never had any trouble being invited back – and distributed. The prisoners were smuggled out a few at a time, and not only from Stalag III. The German authorities were neither stupid nor gullible. They simply trusted Edith and never realised that she was entering the camp with seventeen musicians and leaving with twenty-five.

Only once did she almost come unstuck. This was when she was interrogated by the Gestapo, who accused her of chartering a ship which had been found moored in the docks at Marseilles, obviously ready to transport a cargo of prisoners across the Channel to England. In all probability Edith was responsible for this, and had she not been exonerated she almost certainly would have been shot. Not only did she talk herself out of an exceedingly tricky situation, she gave her interrogators free tickets for her show at Le Perroquet Club, and invited them to the party afterwards!

In all, Edith enabled more than two hundred prisoners-of-war to escape in this way. We do not know for sure if these men were in any real danger. Some probably were homosexuals, and would have received short shrift from the Germans had this become known. Others were friends and acquaintances from her early life in Pigalle and would obviously serve their fellow men better if they returned there to work for the Resistance. Not enough can be said in praise of her exploits during the war. That is why, at her funeral, the French flag was draped over her coffin.

Michel Emer, Edith's lifelong friend and composer, entered her life during the spring of 1940.

She was rehearsing for her new season at the Bobino, that most magical of music-halls, alas now gone, in the rue de la Gaîté. It was the eve of the première. Her secretary announced that there was a young man at the door who wished to offer her a song that he had written especially for her. Tired and impatient, Edith refused to see him. Michel Emer was adamant; he would only go away once Madame Piaf had listened to his song.

Edith relented, out of pity. Michel was an unattractive Jewish boy, with ridiculous bottle-bottom spectacles. But there was something about him which appealed to Edith's better nature. He was wearing a corporal's uniform, and although she did not find him physically attractive, this was a sound enough reason for inviting him in. He told her that he was stationed at the Hôpital Val-de-Grace, off the boulevard de Port-Royal, and that he had been given strict instructions to return there that evening or run the risk of being court-martialled.

Michel Emer sat at Edith's piano and played *L'accordéoniste*. Though he sang badly, she was overwhelmed. The young man had created a masterpiece, words and music! As a songwriter, his fate was sealed. Edith kept him at the piano until five the next morning, determined to sing the song at the Bobino that night. She must have pulled a few strings behind the scenes, too: not only did Corporal Emer go undisciplined, he was also allowed to stay for the opening night.

> La fille de joie est belle,
> Au coin de la rue, là-bas,
> Elle a une clientèle
> Qui lui remplit son bas . . .

> (The prostitute is beautiful,
> On the street corner, over there,
> She has customers
> Who pay her well . . .)

L'Accordéoniste tells the classic story of the forlorn prostitute who spends much of her time standing on the street corner listening to the accordionist. They fall in love and make plans for the future. Then he goes off to war, but does not return. To console herself she goes back on the beat, only to hear another accordionist playing on the same street corner. Unable to stand any more, she screams for him to stop:

> Arrêtez! Arrêtez la musique!

Initially, the song was not a great success. Before the last line the music runs on for several bars whilst the singer buries her face in her hands. The audience were not sure when to applaud. After the Bobino première, however, the song became Edith's biggest hit so far, and it was the first of her records to sell more than a million copies.

Soon afterwards an ever-benevolent Edith paid Michel Emer's way into the unoccupied zone. He returned after the Liberation to write her some thirty songs, all of them hits.

Next in the long line of Piaf songwriters was Henri Contet.

Following the success of *Le bel indifférent*, and probably influenced by Cocteau, the film director Georges Lacombe handed Edith and Meurisse the screenplay for *Montmartre-sur-Seine*. They signed the contract to make the film, and

Edith set about writing the songs for the soundtrack. There would be four, with music by Marguerite Monnot: *L'homme des bars*, *J'ai dansé avec l'amour*, *Un coin tout bleu*, and *Tu es partout*.

> Je te vois partout dans le ciel,
> Je te vois partout sur la terre,
> Tu es ma joie et mon soleil,
> Ma nuit, mes jours, mes aubes claires!
>
> (I see you everywhere in heaven,
> I see you everywhere on earth,
> You are my joy and my sunshine,
> My night, my days, my bright dawns!)

Edith played the leading role in the film, with Meurisse appearing as her co-star. The film prolonged their affair for a few more months. The plot was uncomplicated: Edith was the little flower-seller from Montmartre who fell in love with a working-class boy. The boy was in love with someone else, but the girl managed to cope with her distress by dreaming of one day becoming a famous singer. Part of the story is said to have been based on her earlier relationship with P'tit Louis.

The film was not a commercial success, though it has since become a cult movie amongst Piaf fans, and is often shown in France. What it did was pave the way for Edith's later films, in which she displayed an acting talent once compared with Italy's Anna Magnani. Her admirer in the film was played by none other than Jean-Louis Barrault, who would star a few years later in Marcel Carné's phenomenally successful *Les enfants du Paradis* with Arletty. The publicity poster was drawn by Charles Kiffer, setting what was to be a precedent. Georges Lacombe went on to better things, too: he later directed Gerard Philipe in *Le pays sans étoile*, and Marlene Dietrich in *Martin Roumagnac* in 1946.

Most important of all, however, was Edith's meeting with the film's press attaché, Henri Contet. Edith fell in love with him and immediately nicknamed him Riri, and their relationship brought about some of the most important songs she ever sang.

Henri Contet was also employed by *France-Soir*, and the film magazine *Cinémondiale*. He was handsome, of course, but was already involved with another woman, as Asso had been. This posed no major problem for Edith, who had always adored a challenge, particularly when it came to ensnaring a man.

After shooting *Montmartre-sur-Seine* Meurisse moved out of their apartment, half expecting Henri to move in. He did not. Edith, eternally superstitious and possibly haunted by bad memories, rented another apartment several blocks down the road and just a little closer to the Bidou Bar, a drinking establishment of which she had become inordinately fond. Here she waited for her new lover to move in. Unfortunately for her, and perhaps fortunately for him, Henri stayed put with his woman.

Edith retaliated by attempting to make him jealous. She flirted openly with a young singer, Yvon Jean-Claude. They sang a song together, *Le vagabond*, a lively piece which could definitely be said to mark the beginning of the great Piaf years. In May 1941 Edith also wrote and recorded *C'est un monsieur très distingué*, so obviously aimed at Henri . . .

> Il a aussi un petit chien,
> On dit qu'il fait beaucoup de bien,
> Sa femme, moi, et puis le chien!
> C'est un monsieur très distingué!
>
> (He also has a little dog,
> They say he does things very well
> His wife, me, and then the dog!
> He's a very distinguished man!)

Edith won her battle, eventually, and won Henri's affection. But he never moved in with her; he wrote her a song instead.

For Henri, songwriting was nothing new. Some years before he had written a song for Lucienne Boyer, famous for her gentle, persuasive ballads such as *Dans la fumée* and *Parlez-moi d'amour*. Henri's *Traversée* had been an intensely dramatic piece, not at all in keeping with Lucienne's style. She had taken it out of her repertoire after being hammered by the critics, and Henri had focused his attention elsewhere.

His first song for Edith was *C'était une histoire d'amour*, and even then she flaunted Yvon Jean-Claude in his face by inviting the young singer to stand behind the curtain and sing the last two lines of the refrain:

> Il faut toujours que quelqu'un pleure,
> Pour faire une histoire d'amour!
>
> (Someone always has to cry,
> To make a love story!)

Eventually, because her expenditure far outweighed her income, Edith was forced to leave the new apartment near the Bidou Bar. Her desire to live with Henri Contet was at least partially fulfilled; the songwriter introduced her to Madame Billy, proprietress of the infamous brothel on the rue Villejuste (now the rue Paul-Valéry). The apartment had been cold on account of the fuel rationing, and in truth Edith did not mind where she lived so long as she could keep warm. She stayed with Madame Billy until 1944 when the brothel was closed down by the Gestapo, probably because of Madame Billy's involvement with the black market.

Edith rented the entire third floor, which she shared with Mômone, now welcomed back into the fold, Tchang, Andrée Bigard, occasionally Henri Contet, and a whole host of hangers-on. In her memoirs, Madame Billy speaks lovingly of Edith. Initially, she knew nothing of the singer's bizarre way of life. Edith asked for a piano to be put in her room, and there was another in the salon. Friends came and went, heedless of the curfew imposed by the Germans: Jean Cocteau, Michel Simon, Marie Bell, and Madeleine Robinson . . . these were just a few. Edith rehearsed zealously, or simply entertained her friends, depending on her mood, and almost always in the middle of the night. The neighbours complained to the Gestapo, who did precisely nothing – for two reasons. Firstly, the house was frequented by German officers from their headquarters in the nearby rue Lauriston. Secondly, the enemy *adored* listening to her!

Edith's parents visited her, too. Her father, now registered as unemployed, came weekly and was given food parcels by Madame Billy and money by his daughter. Edith and he were very close. Her mother, according to Madame Billy, and also according to the former mannequin Fabienne Jamet, who ran another *maison*, made a general nuisance of herself. Line Marsa had been in prison for drug offences, and it is said that she even asked Edith once for permission to sing *De l'autre côté de la rue*, one of her biggest songs.

Edith always ignored her mother. She had never forgiven her for deserting her as a baby. Manouche, the celebrated gangster's moll, remembers one incident in particular.

She was at Madame Billy's with Edith, who was singing Mistinguett's *Mon homme*. This is her recollection of it.

Something eerie, even horrible happened. Another voice floated in from the open window. Piaf's voice, and yet not quite Piaf's voice, tremulously singing *Mon légionnaire*, the voice cracked, and somehow dirty. Piaf's face twisted with rage. 'Bitch!' she screamed. She rushed to the window, followed by Cocteau and Manouche. The rue de Villejuste was deserted except for a female figure in red, rocking back and forth. 'Shut her up!' Piaf screamed. Cocteau threw out a ten-franc note. The woman showed her backside, and left . . .

Manouche, who was born Germaine Germain in 1913, became the mistress of the Corsican gangster Paul Carbonne, who was killed by the Resistance. Her biography, written by Roger Peyrefitte in 1972, pulls absolutely no punches. Manouche knew all the controversial stars of the day, including Suzy Solidor and Mistinguett and, like Piaf, she lived life to the full.

It was during her stay at Madame Billy's that Edith first met her brother, Herbert Gassion. Line Marsa sprang the surprise on Louis Gassion by inviting him to a family reunion. When they had separated some twenty years before, Line had been pregnant. The child had been brought up by the Public

Assistance. Exactly how close Edith was to her brother and half-sister is not easily determined. In *Piaf, ma sœur* Denise Gassion published several letters sent by Edith to her and her husband, Roger. As explained above, neither is mentioned in Edith's autobiographies.

During the Madame Billy period Henri Contet was to write some of his best songs, and some of Edith's most memorable. For the moment there were *Monsieur Saint-Pierre*, *Les histoires du cœur*, and the dramatic *Le chasseur de l'hôtel*, all inspired by Edith's riotous lifestyle.

Edith sang at the ABC from 17 October to 12 November 1942. Again, she ended her act with *Oú sont-ils mes petits copains?* complete with tricolour backdrop. This time the implications were more serious. The Gestapo ordered her to remove the song from her repertoire because they considered it to be a blatant mockery of the Third Reich. With incredible nerve, Edith refused, though she did compromise by omitting the tricolour lighting. Incredibly, the Gestapo allowed her to have her own way!

On 30 January 1943 she began a short season at the Folies-Belleville with the artiste then known as *Le chanteur sans nom* – later identified as Roland Avelys. They were to become friends, but not lovers. Avelys was an avid practical joker. Once, when Edith was ill, she appeared on stage and suddenly doubled up as though in pain. Her impresario rushed to her aid, only to be met with the spectacle, in the orchestra pit, of Avelys baring his backside, into which he had inserted a pipe!

On 15 April she appeared in the *Revue des Chansons* at Clichy, and on 10 May was offered a contract to sing at the Vie en Rose, a small cabaret in Pigalle. Five days later she opened at the Casino de Paris, and on 19 May she sang in a gala concert at the ABC with André Claveau, Charles Trenet . . . and Damia, for whom she had written a song, even though she was not yet a member of the Societé d'Auteurs Compositeurs et Editeurs de Musique (SACEM). The song, which had to be signed by Marguerite Monnot, was *Mon amour vient de finir*. Sadly, there is no record of Edith performing it.

Mon amour vient de finir,
Mon amour vient de partir,
Je n'ai plus aucun désir,
Mon amour vient de mourir!

(My love has just finished with me,
My love has just gone away,
I have no more desire,
My love has just died!)

Probably because of pressure of work, Edith dropped out of the *Revue des Chansons* on 6 June and began preparing for yet another season at the ABC.

The 1943 ABC recitals proved more popular than anything she had done before. Accompanied by the Claude Normand Ensemble she opened on 11 June, initially for two weeks. By public demand she stayed a month, singing songs she had written with Marguerite Monnot, and other works by Raymond Asso and Henri Contet. Michel Emer had emerged from exile, briefly, to bring her *Le disque usé*, and the phenomenally successful *De l'autre côté de la rue*.

Des murs qui se lézardent,
Un escalier étroit,
Une vieille mansarde, et me voilà chez moi!
De l'autre côté de la rue y a une fille,
Une belle fille,
Vivre un seul jour sa vie,
Je n'en demand'rais pas plus . . .

(Cracked walls, a narrow staircase,
An old attic, that's my place.
Across the street there's a girl,
A beautiful girl.
I'd ask for nothing more
Than to live one day of her life . . .)

The song was given excellent English lyrics by Christopher Hassall in 1948, under the title 'Just Across the Way'. Edith sang it in the United States, but she never recorded it in English, which is a great pity.

On 3 March 1944 Louis Gassion died at his lodgings on the rue Rebeval, aged sixty-two. Edith was heart-broken. Her one consolation was that he had not died alone; some time before she had supplied him with a manservant, with whom he had spent his last years in his tawdry hotel room.

The funeral, a grand affair, is described by Denise Gassion:

Edith took him (Papa) in her arms. Yvon Jean-Claude was there. He had been touring Switzerland with Edith and had promised to bring Papa some chocolate. Too late, he excused himself by removing his gold cross and wrapping it around Papa's wrist. I will never forget that gesture. Thank you, Yvon.

On Wednesday 8th March at the church of St-Jean-Baptiste in Belleville, the chancel was decked out in black. Even the chairs had been covered and there was a long black carpet up to the altar. It was my [thirteenth] birthday.

The prostitutes from Madame Gassion's brothel in Normandy came to pay their last respects, and all the family was there from Falaise in Normandy. Louis Gassion was buried in the family vault at the Père Lachaise cemetery in Paris. Edith did a recital that night, telling her audience that their applause would be for one man alone, her father.

The following year Edith's mother died of drug addiction, aged forty-seven. She had been living in Pigalle with her lover, André Comès, and the hapless young man, not knowing quite what to do with the body, had moved it to someone else's room and disappeared. By the time the undertaker arrived, it had been shoved into a sack and dumped in the gutter, a fitting end for a pathetic woman.

Edith refused to have anything to do with her mother's funeral, and did not attend it. Henri Contet made all the arrangements; Line Marsa was interred at Thiais, just outside Paris, and at the same time the body of little Marcelle Dupont was exhumed and laid beside Louis Gassion in Père Lachaise.

Edith had been singing professionally for a decade. Her records were selling well and she was earning a lot of money, money which she spent like water. Still there was no regular

impresario to handle her affairs. Off and on she had been
managed by the OSA, an agency which looked after the
affairs of Aimé Barelli, Michel Emer, and the boxer Marcel
Cerdan. The OSA met at the Club des Cinq, their own
haunt in Montmartre. Michel Emer's swing band played
most nights, and there would be guest cabaret performances,
especially from Edith.

Andrée Bigard was looking after what little of Edith's
earnings she could salvage after the revelries, and Edith had
already begun to attract some of the leeches which were to
cling to her in later life. In the spring of 1944 she met Louis
Barrier – quite literally in the street. Loulou, as he soon
became known, was cheeky enough to ask if he could become
her agent. Edith was so bowled over by his nerve that she
agreed, and Loulou represented her for the rest of her life.
When he entered her life he was not a typical impresario,
with thick cigar and flashy car. He was as poor as a church
mouse, and rode around Paris on a bicycle.

Within days of assuming his role, Loulou had secured her
a two-week engagement at that most prestigious of halls, the
Moulin Rouge.

As a matter of course, Edith was allowed to select her
own *vedette-américaine*, the artiste next in line to the main
attraction, preceding the interval. She asked for Roger Dann,
a popular operatic-style *chanteur* of the time, only to be told
that he was working elsewhere. The management of the
Moulin Rouge came up with an up-and-coming young singer
from Marseilles. His name . . . Yves Montand. He was the
first in a long line of entertainers whom she was to befriend,
badger, and nurture towards international success.

Piaf and Montand did not get on at first. A few weeks
before the Moulin Rouge première Edith 'auditioned' him,
such was the weight she carried, and discounting his obvious
good looks, she quickly recognised his potential talent.
Montand was of Italian extraction; he and his family had
fled their country before the war to escape the fascism of
Mussolini. After a variety of jobs he had become a docker,
but his main interest had always been singing. His voice had
a curious, resonant quality and in spite of his youth – he was
just twenty-two – he possessed a better than average stage

presence. On the negative side he wore garish clothes; his gestures were clumsy and contrived; his songs, Edith declared, were uncouth; he sang cowboy songs by the blind composer Charles Humel, and his uncultured Marseilles accent did not help.

When one listens to Montand's pre-Piaf recordings, one wonders if indeed he would have achieved any fame outside Marseilles without her intervention. To correct his accent, she made him sing and speak with a pencil between his teeth. She asked him to discard his jacket, and sing in his shirt sleeves. Finally, she told him to get rid of his dreadful cowboy songs. Liberation was just around the corner, she said. His mock-Americanisms would make him a laughing-stock once the real Americans hit Paris.

Annoyed by her constant criticisms, Montand baptised his mentor a *marchande de cafard* – a merchant of gloom.

Edith asked Henri Contet to write her protégé a new repertoire – not a very thoughtful thing to ask, under the circumstances, for she was falling out of love with the one, and in love with the other. It was a regular Piaf pattern; whenever her current love affair started to turn sour, she always kept the unfortunate man hanging on until a replacement had been found. She hated being alone.

Henri came up with a handful of songs which are still considered Montand classics. *Battling Joë*, the story of the luckless boxer who goes blind; *Gilet Raye*, about the innkeeper who turns convict; *Ce monsieur-là*, about the shy little man who evades the pressures of life by committing suicide. Edith, who had recently passed her SACEM examination by writing a song on the theme *rue de la Gare*, wrote him two songs: *Mais qu'est-ce que j'ai* and *Elle a des yeux*, the latter a clear indication that he was now her lover.

Edith's recitals at the Moulin Rouge were triumphs. Montand's performances attracted only lukewarm applause, and when Loulou Barrier began negotiating contracts for Edith's forthcoming French tour, he suggested that Montand should be placed further down the bill, or dropped altogether. Edith was furious, and refused. For Montand, the tour was a disaster. Three of the venues were Orléans, Lyons, and Marseilles itself – if he had been popular on his home ground once, with a changed style his audiences became hostile towards him. It was a ghastly ordeal; Edith stood by him and he persisted, eventually achieving the success he so richly deserved.

After the tour the pair returned to Paris, where they sang together at the Alhambra. They followed this with a season at the Théâtre de l'Etoile, though by now their personal relationship was beginning to suffer. Edith's discovery had become big business. Few establishments could afford the luxury of Piaf and Montand on the same bill.

As happened with Paul Meurisse, Montand lasted a little longer than expected because of a film he and Piaf made together.

Etoile sans lumière is considered by many to have been Edith's finest film. Its director was Marcel Blistène, a former journalist whom Edith and Andrée Bigard had befriended during the German occupation. For a while he had been hidden at Andrée's farm near Fréjus in the unoccupied zone. Here, he had completed his screenplay with Edith in mind.

The action takes place in 1930. A famous star of the silent screen (Mila Parely) is desperate to resume her career now that the 'talkies' are all the rage. She has, however, failed the voice test. Her director-lover (Marcel Herrand) takes her to his country retreat where she hears the maid (Piaf) singing whilst about her chores. This gives the director an idea. The maid, who is madly in love with a village boy (Montand) is uprooted and offered a job in Paris. Here he raises her hopes of becoming a star by inviting her to sing in front of a microphone, unaware that her voice is being recorded in order to be dubbed over that of the star. The subsequent film is a great success. When the maid goes to see it with her lover, she is shocked to hear her voice singing. The star, filled with remorse over what she has done, commits suicide by crashing her car. The maid returns to the village, to be consoled by her lover.

In the film, Edith again sang *C'était une histoire d'amour*. The other songs, by Marguerite Monnot and Henri Contet, were to be her first pressings for a new contract which she had signed with Pathé–Marconi and which would continue, with two short breaks in 1947 and 1948 when she recorded ten songs with Raymond Legrand and his orchestra for French

RCA, until her death. They were *Le chant du pirate*, *C'est merveilleux*, *Adieu mon cœur*, and the song which tells the ubiquitous story of the woman arrested for murdering her husband, *Mariage*.

> Car tout était miraculeux,
> L'église chantait rien que pour eux,
> Et même le pauvre était heureux!
> Et de là-haut, a toute volée,
> Les cloches criaient, 'Vive la mariée!'

> (It was miraculous,
> The church singing for them alone,
> And even the poor were happy!
> And up there, in full peal,
> The bells cried, 'Long live the bride!'

Etoile sans Lumière was a massive box-office hit in France, and later in the United States, where it played fifty-two consecutive weeks in New York. It launched another international star in Serge Reggiani – soon afterwards he and Montand were a sensation in Marcel Carné's *Les portes de la nuit*. Later, he was to appear with Montand's wife, Simone Signoret, in *Le casque d'or*, and would eventually begin an enterprising career as a *chanteur*, interpreting the songs of Boris Vian and Georges Moustaki.

Edith had more film offers; she turned them down. She was now the Great Piaf, the biggest star in France, and searching for new horizons.

5

The American Gamble

Breaking away from Montand, Edith left Paris for a while, embarking on a tour of Alsace. Accompanying her were a group of nine young singers who called themselves Les Compagnons de la Chanson. Immediately impressed by their vocal technique, she decided to take them under her wing – all nine of them, Albert, Fred, Marc, Jo, René, Guy, Gérard, Hubert and the *patron* of the troupe, Jean-Louis Jaubert.

In 1944, whilst touring Switzerland with Yvon Jean-Claude, Edith had appeared at the Coup de Soleil, a fashionable cabaret in Lausanne. Here, she had listened to Jean Villard, a young *chansonnier*, singing his latest composition, *Les trois cloches*, which he had written under his pseudonym, Gilles. Edith was already familiar with Villard's work; In 1937 she had sung and recorded two of his songs, *Le contrabandier* and *Browning*. Edith liked the song so much that Villard gave it to her, but she did not sing it straight away. The song, she felt, needed a number of harmonising voices. She offered the song to Les Compagnons, who agreed to sing it on one condition, that she sing it with them.

At this time in their career Les Compagnons specialised in folk songs and camp-fire ditties, such as *Pérrine était servante*. *Les trois cloches* was in every sense a *chanson*. It told the story, in simple words, of Jean-François Niçot: his birth, marriage and death in a little village in the heart of a valley. Today it is regarded as pure schmaltz and is not always taken seriously, which is a shame. In 1946, when the record was released, the French looked upon it as a patriotic symbol of peace, a welcome tonic after the ravages of the occupation.

Les Compagnons, with their old-fashioned repertoire, had a limited following. But the potential was there, Edith told them, providing they adopted songs of a more realistic

61

nature. For her it was a terrific gamble. She moved into a new apartment at 26 rue de Berri, and the group moved with her.

Jean-Louis Jaubert became Edith's lover, and the song was a hit.

> Village, au fond de la vallée,
> Comme égaré, presqu'ignoré,
> Voici, dans la nuit étoilée
> Qu'un nouveau né nous est donné!
>
> (A village, deep in the valley,
> Out of the way, ignored,
> Here, one star-filled night
> To us was given a new-born child!)

The song, which had no musical accompaniment whatsoever, opened with Jean-Louis Jaubert singing the verse, which developed into a beautiful crescendo of harmonising voices, through which Edith gradually launched herself into the refrain. For its première she discarded her black dress and chose instead a long, pale blue gown. The shellac recording of the song sold 60,000 copies within three weeks of being released, quite unusual in France in those days. Ironically, Edith had allowed the group to include *Pérrine était servante* on the B side, though she would not sing it with them.

To the English-speaking world Jean-François Niçot became Jimmy Brown, and the song was Edith's ambassador in England and America. Years later she sang it alone, in English, and so did Les Compagnons. They also made other records together: *C'est pour ça*, *La complainte du roi Renaud*, and traditional folk songs such as *Dans les prisons de Nantes*, *Céline*, and *Le roi a fait battre tambour*. None of these ever matched up to the success of *Les trois cloches*, of which Jean Cocteau wrote, 'Piaf's voice is likened to an agate stream, flowing through their bronze and golden bell.'

Suddenly, Les Compagnons de la Chanson were in demand, and had composers writing especially for them. There was George Auric's famous *Moulin Rouge*; the haunting *Mes jeunes années*, by Charles Trenet, and from the pen of Raymond Asso came *Comme un p'tit coquelicot*, though many would argue that the later version of this, by Marcel Mouloudji, was unparalleled. *La Marie*, written for Edith by André Grassi but never performed by her, won them the *Grand Prix du Disque*.

Edith made a film with the group, *Neuf garçons et un cœur*, directed by Georges Freedland. It was shot in less than two weeks, with a very limited budget, and released in 1947.

The plot is relatively simple: a kind of musical fantasy which takes place one Christmas Eve. Edith plays Christine, the leader of a group of penniless singers who are waiting for their dreams to come true. With the help of a kindly benefactor (Lucien Baroux) all ends well. Woven into the plot are the songs: *C'est pour ça* and *Les trois cloches* with Les Compagnons, and solo performances of the self-composed *Sophie*, *Un refrain courait dans la rue* – and *La vie en rose*.

> Quand il me prend dans ses bras,
> Il me parle tout bas,
> Je vois la vie en rose!
> Il me dit des mots d'amour,
> Des mots de tous les jours,
> Et ça m'fait quelquechose!
>
> (When he takes me in his arms,
> He speaks low,
> Life takes on a rosy hue!
> He says words of love,
> Everyday words,
> It does something to me!)

Edith had written both words and music for the song in May 1945. She had been sitting in a café with a singer friend, Marianne Michel, and had scribbled the first few lines on a table-cloth. Though it had been out of character for Edith to even attempt to 'mould' a woman, she had offered her friend *Les choses en rose*. Marianne had suggested substituting *vie* for *choses* because it sounded more romantic.

Publishing the song presented problems. Edith had written songs before, but as she was not yet a member of SACEM the responsibility for the music had always had to be taken on by an established composer. Marguerite Monnot had signed *C'était un jour de fête* and *Un coin tout bleu*. *J'ai qu'à l'regarder* had been signed by Alex Siniavine. None of her regular composers would have anything to do with this one, however. Marguerite Monnot even dismissed it as rubbish. Finally, it was signed by Louiguy (Louis Guigliemi), who had already signed several songs including *C'est un monsieur très distingué*, and *Le vagabond*. The song was recorded by Roland Gerbeau, a well-known charm-singer of the day, and then by Marianne Michel. Edith, who did not care much for the song until someone else had performed it, did not record it until October 1946. Then it took the world by storm.

Immediately after *Neuf garçons et un cœur* Edith and Les Compagnons embarked on a hazardous tour of Greece, hazardous because it was 1946 and the country was in the midst of a general election campaign. The tour was a near-failure, though it did offer her some compensation. After her opening night in Athens she was introduced to a handsome young Greek actor, Takis Menelas.

Their relationship lasted just one week; it seems to have given Edith a taste for Greek men, for there were to be two more. Takis showed her Athens by moonlight. She went with him to the Parthenon on the Acropolis. An incurable romantic, he begged her to relinquish her career and stay with him in Greece. He even offered to divorce his wife and marry her. For Piaf, the adoration of her public was worth much more than the love of a single man, and she refused. Four years later they met again in Paris, and as a tribute to his pretty little *chanteuse* Takis had indeed divorced his wife.

After Greece, Edith took up the greatest challenge of her career – the conquest of the United States.

She was afraid of flying, so she travelled by ship, taking Les Compagnons with her. She opened at The Playhouse on New York's 48th Street in November 1947. Earlier, there had been a welcoming party and press conference at the Ambassador Hotel, where she was staying. An eager young reporter asked her who, in America, she would most like to meet. Tongue-in-cheek she retorted, 'Einstein!' With the help of her ever-faithful friend Jacques Bourgeat, this was arranged.

Her brief season at The Playhouse was a bitter failure. She was not the average American's idea of the French *chanteuse*. They had expected some exotic creature, a kind of white Josephine Baker, wearing gowns by Fath, bedecked in feathers and jewels and singing songs like *C'est si bon*. What they got was a dour little woman clad in black, wearing no make-up, hair dishevelled, and singing songs of lost love and death in a language they could not understand.

These first audiences were shocked – disturbed, even.

Les Compagnons, on the other hand, were an immediate hit with the Americans, who simply adored their uncomplicated camp-fire songs. *Les trois cloches*, which they sang with Edith at the close of their act, had the audiences stamping and whistling in the aisles. For Edith, this was the last straw – did she not know that this behaviour was the supreme accolade, and not an insult. First she ordered her agent, Clifford Fischer, to book her on the next boat home. Then she changed her mind. She had managed to cope with the Germans, and she would conquer the Americans. She was also probably reminded of Yves Montand's dilemma whilst attempting to win over unfriendly audiences during his tour of southern France. Then, she had spurred him on. Here, in a foreign and hostile country, there was no one to give her that essential push. She was on her own. One thing she was certain of, however: she would not return to France a failure.

She began taking English lessons – not only did she learn to speak the language, she taught her English teacher, Miss Davidson, every French obscenity in the book! One night the American theatre critic Virgil Thompson was sitting in the audience. He gave her the big break she had been praying for.

Thompson was a highly respected connoisseur of the arts, and an authority on the *chanson*. Though unaccustomed to writing about music-hall artistes, he devoted two columns to Edith on the front page of *New York Times*:

Miss Piaf presents the art of the *chansonnière* at its most classical. The vocalism is styled and powerful. Her diction is clarity itself. Her phrasing and gestures are of the simplest, save for a slight tendency to over-use the full-arm swing, with index finger pointed. She has literally no personal mannerisms. She stands in the middle of the bare stage in the classical black dress of medium length, her hair dyed red and tousled is equally classical. Yvette Guilbert, Polaire and Damia all wore it so. Her feet planted about six inches apart, she never moves except for the arms. Even with these her gestures are sparing and she uses them as much for abstractly rhetorical as for directly expressive purpose. There is apparently not a nerve in her body. Neither is there any pretext of relaxation. She is not tense, but intense. In no way spontaneous, just thoroughly concentrated and impersonal. Her power of dramatic projection is tremendous. She is a great artiste because she gives you a clear vision of the scene or subject she is depicting, with a minimum injection of personality. Such a concentration at once of professional authority and of personal modesty is no end impressive . . .

It was to some extent due to this article that Edith was offered a contract with the Versailles, that most elegant of New York cabarets, and one of the city's most expensive. It is alleged that Clifford Fischer was so confident of her abilities that he agreed to make good any losses which the management might incur in the event of a failure. As for Les Compagnons de la Chanson, they were touring the United States, playing to packed houses.

Edith dropped the Master of Ceremonies from her act – he had been engaged to introduce and translate each song before she sang it, robbing her act of any sense of continuity; and she began singing in English.

The Versailles was on East 50th Street. For Edith's debut, it was as different from the theatres and cabarets of Paris in the late thirties as anything she could have imagined. Its clientèle were wealthy, and not always easily impressed. Michel Emcr arrived in New York to offer his support – she refused to see him until he had written her a song and he surprised her by coming up with two.

Bal dans ma rue is a lively piece, filled with sounds of the fairground and gaiety. The singer takes her sweetheart to the street celebrations, where she introduces him to her best friend. Later she is bridesmaid at their wedding. *Monsieur Lenoble* is altogether different, a dramatic song about a man who takes too much for granted, including his wife. The wife leaves him for a younger man, and suicide is all that is left to escape the harshness of life. Edith ends the song, typically, by imitating the hissing of the gas tap:

> Monsieur Lenoble se mouche,
> Met sa chemise de nuit,
> Ouvre le gaz et se couche,
> Demain, tout sera fini . . .
>
> (Monsieur Lenoble blows his nose,
> Puts on his night-shirt,
> Turns on the gas and lies down.
> Tomorrow it will be over . . .

The Versailles had booked her for a week; she proved so popular that they kept her on for five months. She broke every conceivable house record and was paid a thousand dollars a week – not that she was interested in how much she earned, only in the fact that at last the Americans had opened their insular hearts.

At the Versailles, Edith met many of the great American show-business legends. Judy Garland, Henry Fonda, Dorothy Lamour, Orson Welles, Lena Horne all came to her dressing room after the show. Interestingly, when one looks at all the publicity photographs taken at this time, Edith appears very un-Hollywood-like, natural, and unaffected by the glamour which she herself admitted to hating. She wears little make-up, no jewellery, no fancy clothes – yet she comes across as more glamorous and certainly more sincere than any of the posers in the pictures.

Only one of these superstars had any impact on her. Marlene Dietrich.

Two women, seemingly with little in common; yet their friendship was to remain solid for the rest of Edith's life. Marlene would marry her, and she would bury her. They laughed together; they cried together. They shared two songs – *La vie en rose*, which even Dietrich was not allowed to sing in France during Piaf's lifetime, and *Le chevalier de Paris*, the latter recorded by Marlene in May 1962, whilst she was in Paris visiting her sick friend.

Marlene, herself essentially a private woman, has said little over the years about her friendship with Piaf. In her autobiography, published in 1984 (though not in English) she says:

> I was terrified of watching her burn the candle at both ends, of seeing her take three lovers at a time. She never realised what she was doing. She was constantly preoccupied by her emotions, by her profession, by her belief in all kinds of peculiarities, by her passion for the universe in general, and for one or two people in particular. She was a fragile bird, but also the Jezebel whose insatiable thirst was made to compensate her insecurity and her self-confessed ugliness. I always respected her attitude and her decisions. I later abandoned her, like a lost child, and I shall eternally regret that . . .

Here, Marlene is obviously referring to Piaf's drink and drug problems.

In a rare act of devotion, Marlene gave Edith her own gold cross set with seven emeralds. With it came a piece of parchment:

> **One must find God**
> **Marlene**
> **Rome, Christmas.**

The talisman became Edith's most prized possession. Such was her faith.

6

Marcel Cerdan: *La belle histoire d'amour*

Edith Piaf and Marcel Cerdan first met at the Club des Cinq in 1946. Their relationship developed slowly. She was otherwise engaged; he was living in Casablanca with his wife Marinette and their three children.

During Edith's season at the Versailles in New York, they met again; this time they fell head over heels in love.

Cerdan was a stocky man, not tall, with a tough face and a mouthful of gold fillings. He was by no means attractive. Known as the Moroccan Bomber, he was the finest boxer France had ever had. He had been born in Sidi-Bel-Abbès in Algeria in 1916, the eldest of five children all of whom, apparently, were mad about boxing. Through his father he had met the trainer Lucien Roupp, who ran a gymnasium. From then on his progress had been astonishing. Young Marcel had won every one of his amateur fights, and between 1933 and 1937 every professional one, too. In January 1939 he fought Harry Craster in London and was disqualified for hitting below the belt. Later that year he won the European Middleweight Championship in Milan. During the war he fought in Italy and Algeria, whilst serving in the French Navy. Of his final record of 113 fights, sixty-six were inside the distance wins and forty-three were won on points. He was disqualified twice and lost only twice – once, it is alleged, because he wanted to give his opponent a lucky break.

For the first time ever, Edith had met her equal, and this was one of the rare occasions when she showed any interest in a man not on her side of the show-business fence. Cerdan was as famous in Europe and America as she was. She could do nothing to further his career other than to love him – this she did with all her heart.

One night after her show Cerdan asked her out to dinner;

he took her to a cheap downtown drugstore, and they ate at the counter. On another occasion he took her to the fair at Coney Island where they were recognised. All the merry-go-rounds ground to a halt whilst she sang *La vie en rose*.

It must be said, however, that the boxer's entourage did not approve of their hero's relationship with Piaf. They considered her bad for his image and a detriment to his professional capacities. The press were secretly bribed into silence; the American public were not as liberal-minded as their French counterparts, and Edith had had a hard enough time winning them over, without provoking a scandal now. Then, in Chicago when Cerdan beat Anton Raadik on points, following this early in 1948 with seven gruelling rounds against Lavern Roach in New York, which he also won, his manager began to believe that perhaps Edith was doing him some good after all.

If anything, Edith passed on her acquired intellectual and cultural qualities to Cerdan, much as she had acquired them from Jacques Bourgeat and Cocteau. Her boxer was a child at heart who loved reading comics. His heroes were Tarzan and the characters of Walt Disney.

Edith made him read Gide's *L'immoraliste* and other great literary works. She bought him the soon-to-be-customary Piaf kit – gold watch and chain, cuff-links and tie-pin from Cartier. She decked him out in a blue suit. In the words of Charles Aznavour, he joined the ranks of 'Piaf's Boys'. Cerdan idolised her; but he always stayed married to Marinette. In *Ma vie* Edith spoke of him intimately for the first time:

> I adored him like a god. I would have done anything for him. Marcel Cerdan transformed my life. Before him I was nothing. Morally, I was a lost cause. I believed that life had no meaning, that all men were animals, that the best thing to do was laugh, drink, and have fun whilst waiting for death to come as soon as possible. Marcel taught me how to live again. He took away the sourness and hopelessness which was poisoning me, body and soul. Even today when I have to make a decision I ask myself: What would Marcel do, in my place?

In May 1948 Cerdan lost his title in Brussels to the Belgian, Cyrille Delannoit, and the press had a field-day. Piaf had brought Cerdan bad luck. A return fight was scheduled to take place two months later. Cerdan regained his title. This time Edith was not at the ringside; she had an engagement in Brussels.

Deliriously happy, she bought a town house at 5 rue Gambetta, in the Bois de Boulogne. It cost her a fortune but it was money well spent she said, because she genuinely believed that she might settle down, after years of flitting from one hotel or apartment to another. The house had a massive living-room, which she wanted to have converted into a gymnasium for Cerdan. For a while she had a great deal of faith in her changed routine. Not that it would ever work . . .

The couple returned to the United States, Cerdan to fight, Edith to take on another season at the Versailles. If the boxer's entourage tried to keep them apart, they failed. Cerdan was in serious training at Loch Sheldrake, a hundred miles or so from New York, for the fight of his career, the World Middleweight Championship against Tony Zale. It is alleged that he hated training, and it is suggested that Edith was smuggled into the camp in the boot of her car because she could not bear being alone. Had this been proved, of course, Cerdan would have been disqualified.

Tony Zale's supporters never took Cerdan seriously. Some of them even sent him threatening letters, warning him what might happen should he be fortunate enough to win the title. Lucien Roupp's attitude towards Edith was far from kind. The American press had broken their vow of silence; now her name spelled bad publicity. If Cerdan lost, it would be because of her.

Mômone, in New York at the time, cashed in on the speculation. She somehow managed to obtain a number of letters which the lovers had written to each other, and in an unexplained though typical act of pure malice, offered them for sale to Cerdan's wife. Then she threatened to expose the truth behind the Piaf-Cerdan romance to the press. Needless to say, she was soon sent packing, though she was at the actual fight, for her photograph appeared in one of the New York dailies, half-smiling, in the company of Edith and Cerdan. The following year, in Paris, she took the couple to court saying that Cerdan had hit her. It came out in court that it was *Edith* who had hit her – and yet, after the hearing, the two women left the court in a taxi, arm in arm and smiling radiantly!

The big fight took place on 28 September 1948 at the Roosevelt Stadium in New Jersey. Cerdan had driven himself to the venue, with Edith and Mômone sitting in the back of his car. The American 'Man of Steel' had already arrived to be greeted by a fanfare of mass hysteria.

Edith sat at the ringside, cheering her champion on, whilst Zale's supporters jeered him. It was a tough fight. By the end of the first round Cerdan was out of breath; by the fourth Zale had practically ended it all. Then, during the twelfth round the champion doubled up in agony and crumpled in a heap on the canvas. Cerdan had won the title.

He returned home to a hero's welcome and was invited to the Elysée Palace to an audience with President Auriol, followed by a state drive through the streets of Paris in an open-topped car. For some reason known only to the boxing profession he had been told that he would only receive his prize money if he had a return fight with the deposed champion. Edith stayed on in New York and finished her season at the Versailles, utterly convinced that her lover's triumph had been yet another of Ste Thérèse's miracles – prior to the fight she had taken him on a pilgrimage to Lisieux. In *Ma vie* she describes both this experience and refers to her close friend, Ginette Richer, with whom she had a platonic relationship.

> I asked heaven for a miracle, and it was fulfilled. I asked Saint Thérèse for nothing for myself – just victory for him. A few days later I was preparing to leave for New York. I was packing my suitcases. My friend Ginette was with me with her husband Michel. A heady scent of roses filled my room. It only lasted a few seconds. Ginette and Michel looked everywhere for a broken bottle of perfume . . . but I knew what it was. My childhood was spent at Lisieux and

I knew that when the Saint was about to grant a favour, she always sent a fragrance of roses.

Edith's harsh methods of working and almost impossible routine often had her entourage sagging at the knees. Her day would begin towards the end of the afternoon, when friends or composers dropped in to pay their respects. The more serious business usually started around midnight. If she was not rehearsing or singing she would be raising merry hell until dawn, by which time she was usually the only one capable of standing on her feet. Even in later life, when she was ill, she was tireless. As Marlene Dietrich says, she really did burn the candle at both ends, and she was utterly ruthless towards anyone who could or would not keep up with her.

During the second half of 1948 she was working harder than ever. There were few songs that year – perhaps the only memorable ones were *Il pleut*, one of the first by Charles Aznavour, *Les amants de Paris*, the only song ever written for her by Léo Ferré, and *Monsieur Lenoble*, which she had brought back from New York. These three songs were included in her new season at the ABC, a gruelling schedule even by Edith's standards – she was performing twice nightly, and there were matinées on most days which meant that she was singing some sixty songs each day.

One evening, after her show at the ABC, she was invited to Carrère's, on the Champs-Elysées. Princess Elizabeth and Prince Philip were in Paris on an official visit, and they had asked to see her. Undoubtedly, it was one of the proudest nights of her life. She sat at the royal couple's table after the performance. In her autobiography she remembers little of the occasion; she was on tenterhooks all night, terrified of making a blunder. It is interesting to note that, though her English was reasonably good, Princess Elizabeth and she spoke only in French. Her songs, carefully selected, had included *La vie en rose*, *Monsieur Lenoble*, *Je n'en connais pas la fin*, and *C'est toi le plus fort*. And when the young princess remarked, casually, that her father the King always enjoyed listening to Edith's records, Edith retorted, 'Fine! I'll send him some!'

In March 1949 Cerdan went to London, where he fought
and beat Dick Turpin at Earl's Court. Edith went with him;
they stayed at London's May Fair Hotel. But she never sang
in Britain, despite pleas from numerous impresarios, and her
visit was as brief as it was secret. There are suggestions that
she sang at a handful of private engagements, but nothing
more.

In April 1949 she worked a three-week stint at the Copacabana, a Brazilian-style cabaret which had just opened in
Paris. Accompanied by David White and his orchestra she
sang his composition, *C'est toujours la même histoire*, and
introduced *Bal dans ma rue* to her French public. She also
sang the first of her two English adaptations of *La vie en
rose*.

> You're too dangerous, chéri,
> Too dangerous for me,
> I know I can't resist you!
> My heart tells me to beware,
> You're dangerous, chéri,
> But I don't care!

It was a poor, over-sentimental version of an already
sentimental song. Edith only ever recorded it on tape, though
it was recorded with some success by Gracie Fields. At about
this time, too, Cerdan appeared in a film called *L'homme
aux mains d'argile*, loosely based on his life. This was the
first of his two films, the other being *Diavolo la Celebrita*.
Edith did not star in the film, but she sang its theme song,
Paris.

Nine months after winning his world title, Cerdan returned
to New York to defend it against Jake La Motta. In the ninth
round, the Moroccan Bomber lost to the Raging Bull.

A return fight was scheduled for the following September,
and for once Cerdan trained rigorously. But when La Motta
injured himself during a training session, the fight was post-
poned until 2 December.

In October, Edith returned to New York. The Versailles,
one of her 'lucky' spots, received her for the third time.
Cerdan, who hated flying, had promised to follow on by
ship. The rest is history. He changed his mind. On 27

October 1949 his plane crashed into Mount Rodonta in the Azores, killing everyone on board. Cerdan was not the only celebrity to die. There was his new manager, Jo Longman, and the world-famous violinist and Piaf's friend, Ginette Neveu.

Cerdan's death will never be explained. No one knows why he took the plane. Was he dreading the long sea journey? Or did Edith telephone him from New York, as has been suggested, begging him to take the plane because she could not endure her loneliness? Or there was another theory – that Cerdan wanted to surprise her by turning up at her opening night at the Versailles.

Alas, we shall never know.

Louis Barrier was the only one who could break the news to Edith, although her friend Marlene Dietrich was close at hand. Edith was devastated. For several days she shut herself up in her room at the Waldorf Astoria and saw no one but those two close friends. As a form of penance, she cut her hair – it was to remain short for the rest of her life. But when Louis Barrier informed her that her performance that night would have to be cancelled, she protested:

'Please, let me sing!'

Coming to terms with her grief, she told her audience that night that she was singing for Marcel Cerdan alone. During the performance she fainted, was revived, and continued singing in one of the most emotional scenes ever seen on an American stage. Next day telegrams and letters poured into the Waldorf Astoria, offering messages of sympathy and encouragement. Andrée Bigard and Jacques Bourgeat flew in from France to be with her, Marlene Dietrich never left her side for a moment.

Cerdan's remains were flown back to Casablanca; he had been identified because he wore a wristwatch on each hand. The French Government awarded him the *Légion d'honneur*, posthumously.

Edith stayed in New York. For her, Cerdan's death clearly marked the beginning of her physical downfall. He would remain the love of her life, more important than either of her two husbands. Had he lived, their love affair would probably have petered out like the others which preceded and followed the Cerdan affair. Edith was too fixed in her ways ever to change. He would have been replaced, especially as most boxing experts had predicted that he would lose the return fight with La Motta. Cerdan was also married, one fact which Edith would have been unable to change, for he had stated quite categorically that he intended to remain so.

So, why was he the love of her life? Quite simply because he had died at the very zenith of their affair.

In memory of her champion, Edith wrote several beautiful songs. The first of these was *Chanson bleue*.

> Je vais te faire une chanson bleue,
> Pour que tu aies des rêves d'enfant,
> Où tes nuits n'auront plus de tourments,
> Tu viendras chanter dans les cieux,
> Chanson bleue!

> (I'm going to sing you a blue song,
> So that you might have a child's dreams,
> And no more tormented nights.
> You'll sing it in the heavens,
> A blue song!)

Marguerite Monnot supplied the music, letting her imagination run wild with an angel choir and violins. For more than a year Edith had regular requiem masses sung for Cerdan in the church at Auteuil, and the masses would end with the choir singing *Chanson bleue*. She sang it live during a French radio broadcast in 1951 and said, 'Of all the songs I've ever sung, *Chanson bleue* is my favourite. I think it will remain so all my life.'

The greatest song in memory of Marcel Cerdan was undoubtedly *Hymne à l'amour*, considered by many ardent Piaf fans to be the finest song she ever sang. She wrote it in December 1949, to Marguerite Monnot's music, and first introduced it to her public in a concert at the Salle Pleyel in Paris in January 1950. It was recorded the following May – her first visit to the Pathé-Marconi recording studio in ten months.

Si un jour la vie t'arrache à moi,
Si tu meurs que tu sois loin de moi,
Peu m'importe, si tu m'aimes,
Car moi je mourrais aussi.
Dieu réunit ceux qui s'aiment!

(If one day life snatches you away from me,
If you die whilst far away,
I won't care, as long as you love me,
For I'll die too.
God unites those who love!)

Hymne à l'amour is the quintessential Piaf – her own personal anthem of pure, unfulfilled love. Her recording of the song sold several million copies, and will sell millions more. There have been countless cover versions in French, mediocre at best, and excellent interpretations in English by Shirley Bassey and Dorothy Squires, who often includes her own personal tribute to Piaf in her act. On the Continent, however, like many Piaf songs, the song still remains Piaf's rightful property, and few artistes may sing it in public without running the risk of severe criticism.

Did Cerdan's death unhinge Edith, temporarily? There are many who think so. Soon after the fatal crash the mother of the dead violinist Ginette Neveu contacted Edith and explained that she had been in touch with her daughter 'from beyond the grave'. Certainly Edith became fascinated by the occult at this time, and bought a *guéridon* – a sort of three-legged table. Assisted by Andrée Bigard and the still-present Mômone, the table was 'tapped'.

To the sceptic, Edith's behaviour may seem incomprehensible. It must be remembered, however, that her grief was so intense and felt by every member of her entourage that her friends would have allowed her to do anything to achieve peace of mind and spirit.

The table followed her everywhere, for several years. She even took it to America on her next tour. The séances appear to have helped her somewhat. They helped others, too, especially Mômone. Besides offering advice the table would ask for money for 'certain people'. And of course, the money always had to be handed over to Mômone for safe-keeping.

Early in 1950 Edith flew to Casablanca to see Marinette Cerdan and her three sons: Marcel, René and Paul. Astonishingly enough the two women became friends. Edith invited the entire family to the house in the Bois de Boulogne, where she pampered them beyond belief. Only she would have had the nerve to do such a thing – she even presented the widow with a rare gift, the mink coat which Cerdan had given her in America.

A few months later the town house in the Bois de Boulogne was sold; Edith lost a lot of money in the deal. This, she declared, was not important. How could she live there now, without Marcel?

7

Aftermath: *La P'tite Lili*

It may be said that Edith Piaf never recovered from Marcel
Cerdan's death. She would mourn him for the rest of her life.
During one of the very first link-ups between New York and
Paris she informed her Parisian audience that with Cerdan
dead, she wanted to die too. Her fans were horrified. They
begged her with one voice not to do it. She had no right to
leave them, they loved her. She belonged to them. Marcel
would have wanted her to fight on.

There was to be no suicide attempt this time. She admitted
herself that she was singing better than ever. And suddenly,
life had taken on a new meaning. She would sing for Marcel,
to promote his memory.

A favourite meeting place for artistes at this time was Le
Petit Club, on the rue Panthieu. Here, during her affair with
Cerdan, she had met the comedian Francis Blanche. He had
written her a fine song, *Le prisonnier de la Tour*. There had
also been a more important meeting, as far as her career
was concerned, with an up-and-coming young singer called
Charles Aznavour.

Aznavour was one half of the Aznavour-Roche duo, and
Edith had already recognised his talents as a songwriter by
singing *Il pleut*. She did tell him, however, that his talent was
being wasted by singing in a duo, and even urged him to go
solo. Moreover, she said that his nose was ugly – no problem,
she added, for it would be reshaped when she took him on
her forthcoming tour of the United States! Aznavour, not
much taller than she was, was immediately fascinated. Soon
afterwards the Aznavour-Roche duo split up.

Aznavour has always maintained that he was madly in
love with Piaf for a week. She never fell in love with him
at all – only with his songs. At first he became an essential

part of her household, running errands and answering the telephone, carrying suitcases, driving the car, and helping out backstage, enjoying every moment as general factotum to the woman he had come to idolise.

Edith did not sing many Aznavour songs. Unlike Henri Contet, Louiguy, Marguerite Monnot and Michel Emer, her 'regulars', Aznavour's songwriting phase for Piaf lasted only a few years. Their close friendship lasted all her life. In 1951 when she was preparing to launch herself into the untried field of musical comedy, she accepted no fewer than five of his songs. These were *C'est un gars*, *Il y avait*, *Poker*, *Plus bleu que tes yeux*, and the ominous *Une enfant*.

> Une enfant, une enfant de seize ans,
> Une enfant du printemps,
> Couchée sur le chemin,
> Morte . . .
>
> (A child, a child of sixteen,
> A child of springtime,
> Lying beside the road,
> Dead . . .)

Aznavour also adapted the Wayne Franklin song, 'Jezebel', a big hit in England and the United States for Frankie Laine. Edith's version, one of her most difficult songs with its wide range, was almost as popular in America as the original. But when Aznavour offered her *J'ai bu* and *Je hais les dimanches*, Edith promptly turned them down. The first song, she said, was too masculine. The other she disliked because it condemned Sundays. Aznavour himself had a big hit with *J'ai bu*; he offered *Je hais les dimanches* to Juliette Greco, darling of the existentialists, and then as now one of France's most respected singers. Greco put it into her repertoire and it is still there. It was a massive success. Edith was furious, though she was kind to Greco. She waited until the end of 1951 before recording the song herself.

Now there was another man in her life. Early in 1950 Edith had been singing at the Baccara in Paris, when a young American approached her with an English translation of *Hymne à l'amour*. His name was Eddie Constantine. Edith accepted the song; she and Constantine became friends.

By 1951 they were lovers.

Eddie Constantine had been born into a family of entertainers in October 1915. He won a prize for singing bass at the Vienna Conservatoire, since which time he had earned his living with a variety of jobs, from advertising chewing-gum to helping out at a funeral parlour. He had left his wife and daughter to come to Paris, hoping to make his fortune. Lucienne Boyer had signed him up to appear at the Club de l'Opéra, where he sang with Léo Marjane and Suzy Solidor.

With Piaf – or through Piaf – he became a star.

Edith fell for him in a big way. She was still living at her town house, and he moved in with her. In a rugged sort of way he was good-looking, with a scarred, pock-marked face, a winning smile, and an affable disposition. Edith, whose command of the English language was acceptable, made him learn French. She was preparing for her fourth trip to the United States, to be preceded by a two-month tour of France. She had already signed up Aznavour to open the show. Naturally, there would have to be a spot for Constantine, too.

The French tour was a triumph for Edith, but a trial for everyone else. Between it and America there was a lightning tour of Canada. And as usual, Edith's first port of call in New York was the Versailles. Here she was invited to General Eisenhower's table. A few months later, of course, he would be elected President. At Eisenhower's request she sang *Les feuilles mortes*, another standard which ironically had been launched by Montand and Greco, and *Simply a Waltz*, the only song she never sang in French. Eisenhower declared this to be his favourite song of all time.

> When they start playing the waltz
> That goes round and round
> Like a merry-go-round in the spring,
> With the music swaying,
> I start to dream . . .

Returning to Paris, she paid a brief visit to Marinette Cerdan in Casablanca. Then she threw herself wholeheartedly into her next big venture, the musical comedy, *La P'tite Lili*.

The play has a chequered history. Mitty Goldin of the ABC had commissioned Marcel Achard of the Comédie Française to write the play, and Achard had created its heroine with Edith in mind. His idea was that the dialogue should be witty and the songs sad and dramatic. In any case, most of them had been written already. *Du matin jusqu'au soir*, with words and music by Edith, had been in her repertoire for a while; she had sung it in English at the Versailles in 1950. The other songs included *Rien de rien*, by Aznavour and Roche, *C'est toi*, again written by Edith and one of her two duets with Constantine, who naturally had to be included in the production, and *Petite si jolie*, the song which she had written for Constantine to sing alone. The remaining songs were written by Marcel Achard, with music by Marguerite Monnot. First of all, though, there were many difficulties to overcome.

Edith adored the ABC, the scene of so many of her earlier triumphs. True, Mitty Goldin was not the easiest person in the world to get on with, but neither was Edith. Determined to have the play produced at the ABC, she asked a friend, Raymond Rouleau, to produce it. Lina de Nobili, an enterprising young artist, was engaged to design the set.

There were terrible clashes of personality. Raymond Rouleau would have nothing to do with the playwright or the director. Mitty Goldin flatly refused to have Lina de Nobili anywhere near his theatre, let alone inside it. In fact, the only person upon whom everyone agreed was Marguerite Monnot. Edith fought to restore calm, with some success. Then Achard dropped his bombshell. The play which had caused so much heartache, had not even been written!

Rehearsals took six weeks. Each morning the cast would gather around Achard to read what he had written the night before, and no one knew the identity of the murderer until the very last moment. Then there were more problems. Edith had insisted upon Eddie Constantine playing the part of the gangster, Spencer, but as his French was appalling and his acting even worse, Raymond Rouleau cut out most of his lines and Mitty Goldin would not pay him the salary that Edith insisted on. Another problem concerned the part of Mario, Edith's lover in the play. The part had been given to the songwriter Pierre Destailles, but after all the wrangling, he was now unavailable. Edith suggested the young comedian, Robert Lamoureux. He was tall and handsome, young and talented, just right for the role of Mario. What she did not add was that she was madly attracted to him. He had visited her house several times, offering her songs – always a good ploy. The songs she had rejected, though Lamoureux had become a close friend. He was readily accepted by Raymond Rouleau, who next turned Constantine's part into a silent one.

Edith flew into a rage and threatened to drop out of the production altogether. Mitty Goldin retaliated by threatening to sue her for breach of contract, and the ensuing scene in the director's office, and Edith's words, are unrepeatable. Needless to say, she won her battle: Constantine kept his lines, though Edith made up the difference in his salary. Mitty Goldin walked out and did not enter his own theatre for a week, and it was some time before he spoke to Edith again; for the rest of his life he would dislike her.

La P'tite Lili took Paris by storm, breaking only when Edith was badly injured in a car crash. As with Meurisse and Montand, it served to prolong her affair with Eddie Constantine, already beginning to sour. The plot of the play is uncomplicated. Lili works for a grand couturier, and is madly in love with the porter, Mario. The curtain rises to reveal a stage divided into three. Spencer's beautiful girlfriend (played by the former mannequin, Praline) is being pinned into a gown by Lili, who begins singing *Avant l'heure*. During the course of the play she is fired for singing too much and not working enough. She meets Spencer, lately involved in a murder, and goes to live with him. After he deserts her she decides to kill herself. Fortunately the pharmacist prescribes for her a fake poison which gives her the will to live again. She and Mario are subsequently reunited, and the play ends happily.

Both Robert Lamoureux and Eddie Constantine went on to better things because of the play. The former became one of his country's top comedians. Constantine made countless gangster films in Europe and America, and is well known for his tough-guy image. In his autobiography, *This Man is Not Dangerous*, he sings Edith's praises.

> She gave me confidence in myself when I had no confidence. She gave me the will to fight when I did not want to fight. In order for me to become someone she made me believe that I was someone . . . she had a kind of genius for strengthening and affirming my personality. Time and time again she told me, 'You've got class, Eddie. You're a future star!' Coming from her, a star of the highest order, that was enough. It gave me new life.

For Edith, *La P'tite Lili* was a personal success attributable to her extraordinary willpower and conviction. The critic, Ribadeau-Dumas, writing for the magazine *Paris-Théâtre* justifiably pointed out:

> Ten ravishing songs by Marguerite Monnot, a masterly production by Raymond Rouleau and an exquisite decor by Lina de Nobili, painted in dreamy colours on gauze as fine as butterfly wings. A long time ago I considered Edith Piaf as the greatest artiste of her time. Her voice, grave and overwhelming, plunges me into an ice-bath and gets at my very core. Until now I had one small doubt. How would she face up to this new challenge? Simple! From the very first moment Edith Piaf asserts herself as a marvellous actress. The music-hall is decidedly a famous conservatoire!

Max Favalelli, writing for *Paris-Presse*, concluded:

> *La P'tite Lili* IS Edith Piaf. Marcel Achard wrote this story for HER. Tender, rosy, grey and sweetened with the perfume of cornflowers.

Besides *C'est toi*, the piece gave Edith two commercial successes, *Si, si, si*, sung with Constantine, and the profoundly optimistic *Demain il fera jour*:

> Demain, il fera jour!
> C'est quand tout est perdu que tout commence!
> Après l'amour un autre amour commence!
> Tu vas sourire encore,
> Aimer encore, souffrir encore, toujours!
> Demain!

> (Tomorrow will be another day!
> It's when all is lost that everything begins
> After love another love begins
> You will smile again,
> Love again, suffer again, always!
> Tomorrow!)

Throughout her life Edith remained an intensely superstitious woman. Before going on stage she always performed the same ritual. She would make the sign of the cross and kiss the talisman she always wore. She would touch or kiss the floorboards. Finally, she would make a curious gesture using her little and forefinger, forming them into the horns of her 'imaginary demon'. She also had her 'days'. Thursdays were important. She had met Cerdan on a Thursday; she would later marry on that day. Whenever possible, she would only sign a contract on a Thursday. Sundays, on the other hand, were unlucky:

> Tous les jours d'la semaine
> Sont vides et sonnent le creux,
> Mais y a pire que la semaine,
> Y a l'dimanche prétentieux.
> Je hais les dimanches!

> (Every day of the week
> Is empty and hollow.
> But worse than the week,
> Is pretentious Sunday.
> I hate Sundays!)

Besides the countless table-tapping sessions, she also made regular visits to her clairvoyant. It was on one such occasion that she was forewarned of her two bad car crashes. Colours were important, too. Violet was her favourite – she had worn Yvonne Vallée's violet silk scarf during her first performance at Gerny's. Green was to be avoided at all costs. The mannequin, Praline, had turned up at rehearsals for *La P'tite Lili* wearing a green coat; soon afterwards she had been killed in a car crash.

The play ran successfully for seven months, by which time Eddie Constantine had been replaced in Edith's affections by the racing cyclist, André Pousse.

She and Pousse had first met at the Versailles in 1949, having been introduced by Louis Barrier. At that time there had been no chance of a romantic attachment because she had been with Cerdan. Pousse had been racing at New York's Madison Square Garden with his team-mate, Francis Grauss.

During the summer of 1951, reckless as ever with her spending, and acting on the pretext that the country air would do her good, Edith bought a farm, Les Cerisiers, at Hallier, near Dreux. It cost fifteen million *anciens francs* – five years later it would be sold for little more than half of this. Though like a fish out of water whenever she was away from Paris, Edith would snatch the occasional weekend at her country retreat.

It was after one such rendezvous that she invited Pousse back to the house in the Bois de Boulogne. He stayed for more than a year.

Like Cerdan, Pousse was a star in his own right. He was given the full Piaf treatment. She had ideas of turning him into a singer, even planning a revival of *Le bel indifférent*. She wanted him to make a comeback on the racing track, and offered to buy him a racing car. Pousse refused to be manipulated.

On 24 July 1951 Edith's Citroën crashed into a telegraph pole not far from the farm. Aznavour was driving. The car was a write-off, but amazingly the couple escaped with little more than cuts and bruises. Three weeks later Pousse was at the wheel. It was eight in the morning. Edith and Aznavour were asleep in the back of the new car when it skidded off the road near Tarascon. This time she was not so lucky. She fractured her left arm and broke two ribs.

She was taken to a local hospital and patched up. The play was nearing the end of its run, and for several nights she performed with her arm in a sling. The tight casing around her rib-cage caused her excruciating pain, especially when she sang – and she had to sing, otherwise life would have had no meaning. In order to cope with this, she was prescribed morphine injections, on which she became increasingly dependent until, in a very short time, she was injecting herself through her clothes, with unsterilised needles. This, and the fact that she was still suffering the effects of Cerdan's death, made her more vulnerable than ever. Drug peddlers made a fortune out of her, and so did some of her so-called friends – Mômone, particularly. Her true friends, of course, watched her carefully. She outsmarted the best of them by hiding drugs everywhere they never thought of looking.

This was Piaf's second dark period. Incredibly, it produced some of her finest songs: *Padam padam* by Norbert Glanzberg and Henri Contet, *La rue aux chansons* and the ingenious *Télégramme* by Michel Emer, and by Gilles, *A l'enseigne de la fille sans cœur*:

> Dans ce p'tit bar, c'est là, c'est là qu'elle règne,
> On voit flamber sa toison d'or.
> Sa bouche est comme un fruit qui saigne,
> Mais on dit que son cœur est mort!
>
> (In the little bar, it is there that she rules,
> You see her shock of blazing golden hair.
> Her mouth is like a bleeding fruit,
> But they say that her heart is dead!)

In *Ma vie* Edith remembers the car crash, and how she was still mourning the greatest love of her life:

> On the eve of my death I will be thinking about a song. And if I could choose, I would rather collapse on stage and never get up again. I had a car accident near Tarascon. I

have often regretted that it did not kill me. I would have joined one [Cerdan] whom I could never manage to forget . . .

The accident more or less ended Edith's involvement with André Pousse, though not before he had smashed her 'table' with his bare hands.

Whilst Pousse was at the house in the Bois de Boulogne, she fell for his best friend, Louis (Toto) Gérardin, a fellow cycling champion who had visited her whilst she had been in hospital. Pousse moved out . . . Gérardin moved in – leaving his wife and taking most of the family valuables with him, including several championship trophies, jewellery, precious porcelain, a mink coat, most of the money from the family safe, and no fewer than eighteen gold ingots.

In December 1951 Toto's wife, Alice, hired a private detective and had the couple followed. Edith was openly accused of receiving stolen goods, and her name made headlines throughout Europe. The police, who had been waiting since 1936 to get even with her, interrogated her. The press had a field day. She retaliated by throwing Gérardin out into the street.

She moved into an apartment on the boulevard Péreire. Though she did not know it, she had already begun her descent into hell.

8
The Years of Hell

Edith Piaf and Jacques Pills had first met in the corridors of Radio-Cité in 1939. She had been taking her first hesitant steps at the ABC. He had been at the height of his career as one half of that celebrated duo, Pills and Tabet, known mostly for their interpretations of songs by another famous pair, Mireille and Jean Nohain. They were known for one song especially, *Couchés dans le foin*, recorded in English as *Lazing in the Hay* and later also recorded by the Andrews Sisters.

In 1939 neither of them had been free. Edith had been in the middle of her stormy affair with Paul Meurisse; Pills had been married to Lucienne Boyer. They had met again during the war, whilst Edith had been touring with Cocteau's play. Naturally, they had become friends. Pills was known for his easy-going manner and ever-ready smile. He was nicknamed Monsieur Charm. But until 1952, any relationship between these two great artistes remained platonic.

In May 1952 Pills returned from an American tour and presented her with a song, *Je t'ai dans la Peau*.

> Je t'ai dans la peau,
> Y'a rien à faire,
> Obstinément tu es là,
> J'ai beau chercher a m'en défaire,
> Tu es toujours près de moi!
>
> (I've got you under my skin,
> Nothing can be done,
> Stubbornly, you are there,
> I've tried hard to rid myself of it,
> You're always close to me!)

Pills had written the words. The music had been composed by his pianist, François Silly. It was such a personal lyric, which Edith interpreted in just the way Pills had intended. She fell in love with the song, and the man. Her recording of *Je t'ai dans la peau* is the most suggestive song she ever sang, perhaps with the exception of *Dany* which she recorded in 1949, and was a kind of forerunner to the sexy Jane Birkin-Serge Gainsbourg duets of the late 1960s and early 1970s. Soon afterwards François Silly changed his name to Gilbert Bécaud, and yet another international entertainer was launched. Becaud and Piaf collaborated on two songs, *Elle a dit* and *Et ça gueule-ça madame* – the latter a duet with Pills.

For Edith, it was love at first sight; for two weeks she did not let him out of her sight. He was kinder, more patient and more attentive than any man she had known since Cerdan. She, with her habit of shortening names, now became his Didou. Pills proposed to her – though it has often been said that it was she who proposed to him. The couple were formally married at the Mairie of the 16th arrondissement on 29 July 1952. Edith Giovanna Gassion became Madame René Vitor Eugène Ducos. She was thirty-six, he ten years older. He had lied to her about his age, afraid that she might turn him down because of the age difference.

For Edith, however, there could be no true marriage without a choir and church bells. Her 'real' wedding took place in New York on 20 September 1952, at the Church of Saint Vincent-de-Paul. Louis Barrier and Marlene Dietrich were witnesses . . . Marlene was a non-Catholic, and Edith saw to it that a special dispensation was obtained. Marlene arranged practically everything, from the bouquet of white rosebuds which she bought for the bride, to controlling the behaviour of the throng of press and photographers within the church. Edith wore a long, pleated pale blue gown and a violet tulle hat. After the ceremony there was a reception at the Versailles, followed by a spectacular luncheon at Le Pavillon, one of New York's most exclusive restaurants.

There was to be no honeymoon; Edith was singing at the Versailles, and Pills had a contract with La vie en rose, a fashionable night-club which had been named in honour of Edith's biggest hit in America.

Leaving New York, the newly-weds toured together, performing in San Francisco, Las Vegas and Hollywood – in separate auditoria, of course. They saw little of each other between shows. In Hollywood she met Charlie Chaplin, a rare occurrence for a man who had often confessed a dislike of music-halls and cabarets. Edith found 'Charlot' fascinating, and was probably reminded of the times she and P'tit Louis had watched his films in Montmartre. She remembered him with great reverence, and with a confusing excess of respect when one considers that she was as great in her field as he was in his. Chaplin invited her to stay at his home in Beverly Hills, and he even promised to write her a song – a promise he could hardly keep, for Edith's was a highly portentous, totally individual style, not at all in keeping with his own.

Then Edith and her husband returned to their new apartment in Paris.

67 boulevard Lannes was to remain Edith's home for the rest of her life, of which little more than decade remained. The most incredible thing was, she never really moved in! It was a large, stylish apartment with nine rooms, but as far as she was concerned the only rooms of any importance were the kitchen, the bathroom, her bedroom, and the ballroom-sized lounge. Here she installed a grand piano, several tables which were eternally cluttered with glasses and manuscripts, divans and armchairs for those of her entourage who could not keep up with her to flop into, and trunks: Edith was always on the move and there was no need, she thought, ever to unpack them.

The evenings at the boulevard Lannes were renowned. Edith had an enormous zest for life and was utterly indefatigable, even towards the very end. Before a show or tour she would fling herself heart and soul into her work, caring little for the creature comforts of her fellows; if she could do it, so could they. There was no escaping her tyranny. New songs were rehearsed and rehashed with fervour. She was known to work solidly from dusk until dawn perfecting a single song. Because she was a perfectionist, she demanded nothing less from her composers. Michel Emer, Henri Contet and Marguerite Monnot had already adapted their lives to please her. Others were forced to follow suit. Some wanted to because they admired her; others forced themselves to because they were bleeding her dry. Pierre Delanoë, Michelle Senlis and Claude Delécluse, Jacques Larue, Philippe Gérard and Jean Dréjac were all working for her now.

Edith and Pills were in love. Yet the four years of their marriage were Edith's nightmare.

The marriage was probably doomed from the start. Edith, perpetually in search of that security which had always somehow evaded her, had drifted uncompromisingly from one man to the next. Had her life been less complicated, there would have been fewer songs, for most of her songs spoke of her experiences. Pills, with his casual manner and sympathetic charm, might have made the ideal husband had he been a little more persuasive. Edith needed an iron hand to guide her back onto the rails. Pills was weak. She lied to him about her addiction to drugs, maintaining that the morphine and cortisone injections had been prescribed for rheumatism – she had suffered a bad attack of this in 1949. Initially, Pills believed her. As far as her drink problem was concerned, he was more a companion than a moderator. Some of their binges were as notorious as the ones with Yvonne de Bray. In 1970, when interviewed for *I Regret Nothing*, Pills spoke cheerfully of how he had been proud to be Piaf's husband, even if he had never become 'Monsieur Piaf'. Tragically, he died before the film was completed.

From a professional point of view, they were totally incompatible. Establishments able to afford Piaf and Pills were few and far between, though Edith was loath to appear without him, once she had resettled in Paris. Disregarding the viability of the project, she decided to do a series of double recitals with her husband. It was the biggest financial disaster of her career, and almost killed her reputation as the greatest *chanteuse-réaliste* of the century.

The first half of each show had Piaf and Pills singing together. After the interval there was a revival of *Le bel indifférent*, with Pills playing the difficult role of Emile, so wonderfully created by Paul Meurisse.

First, she decided she would rid herself of the drug problem.

The detoxication affected her badly. At the clinic the doctors began by administering the number of injections she had become accustomed to – as many as eight per day. Day by day, the doses diminished until they ceased altogether. She went almost insane with the pains which racked her frail body. She lost weight, not that she had ever had much to spare. After just three weeks, she returned to the boulevard Lannes. Her physician, Doctor Migot, forewarned her of the depression which was almost certain to follow the cure. In order to cope with the depression, she began taking drugs again.

For the first time ever, her public questioned her credibility. She sang *Les croix*, a number by Gilbert Bécaud which summed up her life at that time, for she was indeed carrying an immense leaden cross. She was hardly strong enough to stay on her feet for a full performance, and during the gala shows running up to her new venture, disappeared regularly into the wings to inject herself, so much so that few theatre managers would accept responsibility for her. In fact, no one at all would stage the double shows with Pills, a matter she resolved by personally booking the Théâtre Marigny in Paris. By this time the format of the recitals had been changed. Pills would open the show, and she would close it. *Le bel indifférent* would be sandwiched awkwardly between.

Edith spent lavishly on the production, money she could ill afford. She imported two mandolinists from Florence, possibly the same ones who are heard on her May 1953 recording of *Les amants de Venise* Her new songs included that number, *Sœur Anne*, *N'y va pas Manuel* and *Et moi*, all by Michel Emer. But apart from these, all the dramatic songs had been removed from her repertoire. The result was a 'syrupy' Piaf, ill-favoured by the critics, and despaired of by her baffled audiences.

Of course, no problem was too tough for her to cope with. The drugs saw to that. The critics murdered her. Pills was hopeless in the play, even with a silent part. It closed after just one month, much to everyone's relief.

The couple toured the provinces in 1954, and Edith began drinking again – heavily. This affected her performances. In Lyons she was whistled at. On another occasion she was too drunk to stand, and the curtain was brought down. At Royat she was jeered at because she forgot the words to *Le chant du pirate*. Instead of singing *marchant par-dessous les tempêtes* (marching under storms) she sang *marchi les blaches gourmettes* (untranslatable).

After the tour there was another visit to the detoxication clinic, but Edith discharged herself after a few days to prepare for a gruelling ninety-day tour with the SuperCircus. Pills went with her, and for the first time ever she sang under a massive marquee, not unlike the set-up for the recent Barbara recitals in Pantin. By this time a massive proportion of her earnings was being doled out to drug peddlers, and she was constantly hounded and threatened by the press. To make ends meet she sold her farm, along with several oil paintings and much of her jewellery – not that she had ever worn much of this, for few of her 'off-duty' photographs show her adorned with anything more than her talisman, or her 'lucky' rabbit's foot.

In *Ma vie* she speaks of the sale of Les Cerisiers with humour:

> I told myself that I wanted to breed cows. It was all the rage . . . all the artistes were going into breeding. But in four years I picked two kilos of green beans, a pound of strawberries . . . and some tomatoes. I bred two chickens, a rabbit, and all the cats in the neighbourhood.

The SuperCircus tour ended at Cholet. One of Edith's last songs was *Bravo pour le clown!* by Louiguy, perhaps the most successful song he ever wrote. Despised by his son, and nagged by his wife, the clown kills the wife and ends up in a lunatic asylum. It is a very dramatic piece, suggestive of her early life with her father, and is one of the few *impersonal* numbers which may not justifiably be sung by anyone else:

> Je suis roi et je règne. Bravo!
> Venez, que l'on m'acclâme,

J'ai fait mon numéro,
Tout en jetant ma femme
Du haut du chapiteau! Bravo!

(I am king, and I rule. Bravo!
Come, how I am acclaimed,
I've done my bit
In throwing my wife
From the top of the tent! Bravo!)

As a last resort, Louis Barrier stepped in and whisked her off to a clinic. It was an act of pure devotion, from the heart. Edith was putty in his hands because she trusted him more than any living soul. Her circle of friends was not inexhaustible; close friends could be counted on the fingers of one hand. Charles Aznavour, well on the road by now towards eternal stardom, had been replaced as factotum by a young man called Claude Figus.

Today, Claude Figus would be regarded as a 'groupie' – a stage-door Johnny who had more or less pestered his way into her entourage and who had remained there because of his unselfish devotion and absolute commitment to the woman he had idolised since childhood. He was also a bad influence; during the worst part of her alcoholism he had helped her to hide cans and bottles all over the apartment, and had never participated in any of the regular 'bottle-searches' conducted by her more responsible friends. Of course, Edith would never be outdone. If all else failed she would simply throw a coat over her night-dress and go out in search of a bar. No one ever refused to serve Edith Piaf, even if they were closed. Usually, Figus accompanied her. He was a strange little man of ambiguous sexuality, although he did boast several years later that he had been her lover, albeit briefly.

Edith pulls no punches when describing her last day at the detoxication clinic. In *Ma vie* she says:

It must have been the longest and most horrible day my life. I bawled like a lunatic and chewed the curtai I writhed on my bed in agony. I foamed at the mouth but I wanted to be cured! Dr Migot asked me if I wanted one last shot. Suddenly, I saw my mother's face. My poor, feeble mother whom I tried four times to detoxicate. Who each time fell back on her vices . . .

In this respect, she was little stronger than Line Marsa had been. But the cure for alcoholism was infinitely worse. According to Edith, she only endured it because of a vision:

My little girl, Marcelle, appeared to me in my sleep. She was crying. I told myself that it was I, her mother, who had made her cry . . .

Edith emerged from the clinic almost cured – almost, because she immediately followed her doctor's orders by going on a diet of fruit: melons in port wine, and pineapples and strawberries in kirsch. The drug peddlers plagued her, too, though by this time she was sensible enough to send them packing.

Louis Barrier had secured her another contract with the Versailles in New York. Composers were busy on both sides of the Atlantic, writing new songs and translating or adapting old ones into English. The Great Piaf was back in full swing. This time there would be no stopping her. At the same time, Pills was in the middle of rehearsals for his new musical play, due to open in London. They were about to go their separate ways.

During this disastrous period there was at least some success. In 1952 she was awarded the *Grand Prix du Disque* for *Le chevalier de Paris*, a delightful piece by Angele Vannier and Philippe Gérard. The prize was presented by Colette and Edouard Herriot, with a great deal of publicity. The song, whilst not a great international song for Edith, did achieve later notoriety thanks to German versions by Marlene Dietrich and Hildegarde Kneff, and it was a hit in English for Peggy Lee, who also sang *If You Go*, an English translation of *Si tu partais*. A year earlier, Edith had won the *Concours de Deauville* with *La chanson de Catherine*.

There were also cameo roles in three films. *Si Versailles ‑ait conte* was directed by that great entrepreneur of the

Piaf with Lena Horne, 1948

Piaf with Marcel Cerdan and Mathilda Nail, 1949

Piaf and Pills at their wedding in New York in September 1952. Marlene Dietrich is on the left of the picture with Ginette Richer on Pills's right

Piaf in front of the church of Notre Dame, 1954

Piaf at her farm, 1958

Piaf at her farm 1958

Piaf with her first husband, Jacques Pills, rehearsing for Olympia '55

Piaf and friends in a relaxed mood. Charles Dumont is on
the right of the picture with Francis Lai on the left

Piaf in the American hospital shortly before making
her comeback at the Olympia, 1960

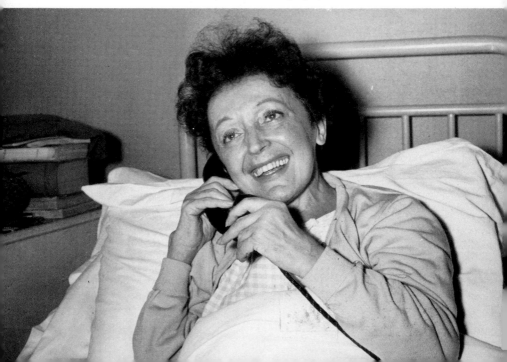

On stage at the Olympia, 1961

Singing *Les blouses blanches*

Piaf and Théo Sarapo in Cannes after announcing
their engagement, July 1962

Piaf and Théo Sarapo at the American hospital at Neuilly, 1962

Singing La foule

French cinema, Sacha Guitry. Guitry's idea, which proved successful, was that all the major roles in his film should be played by minor stars, and that famous names should play only cameo roles. Edith sang Le 'Ça Ira', and though as always the first take was the best, Guitry later admitted that he had made her go through the song several times because he was enthralled by her singing.

In Renoir's French Can-Can, which told the story of the birth of the Moulin Rouge, Edith interpreted the role of Eugènie Buffet, a popular but underrated singer who rose to prominence singing in the streets, like Piaf, at the turn of the century. The song was La sérénade du pavé.

Finally, Boum sur Paris was a fascinating musical extravaganza with a somewhat flimsy plot. Bottles of perfume are given out at a musical celebration, one of which contains an explosive, hence the film's title. During the search for this bottle, many famous stars are encountered, including Mouloudji, Juliette Greco, Piaf and Pills, Lucienne Delyle and Charles Trenet.

By the end of 1954 Edith's career was more settled than it had been for some time, although she still had some way to go as far as overcoming her drug and drink problems was concerned. Then, unexpectedly, she attained unimagined heights. Louis Barrier secured her a contract with the Paris Olympia.

The Olympia has a long history. In 1893 it had been called Les Fantaisies Oller, after its inaugurator, Joseph Oller. Before 1928 some of France's most famous names had appeared there, including the great clown, Grock, and of course Damia. Then it had been turned into a cinema under the direction of Jacques Haik. In 1954 it was taken over by Bruno Coquatrix, an acquaintance of Edith's who quickly became one of her closest friends.

The Olympia was, and still is to a certain extent, the most important music-hall in France. Until Coquatrix' death in April 1979 its placards boasted a galaxy of international stars: Brel, Brassens, Judy Garland, Marlene Dietrich and Josephine Baker all starred there. And the stars of today continue the tradition: Amalia Rodrigues, Leo Ferré, Barbara, Nana Mouskouri, Bécaud, Aznavour, Petula Clark . . .

Initially, Coquatrix hesitated about booking Piaf. Newspapers and journals rarely shrank from reporting episodes from her 'deplorable way of life', and the disastrous tour with Jacques Pills must also have been at the back of the impresario's mind. But he finally signed her up for just one month – even that was twice the length of a normal contract. She opened in January 1955, only to prove beyond doubt that she was the hottest property in France.

The recitals incorporated many of the Piaf classics, along with new material by René Rouzaud, Henri Contet, and of course Marguerite Monnot. Her opening number was *Heureuse*, inspired by her marriage and publicly proclaiming her most sacred vows, though she was far from happy at the time. There were revivals of *Je n'en connais pas la fin* and *L'accordéoniste*, and *Y a pas de printemps* was sung with additional lyrics: the recorded version of 1944 was two minutes shorter. *La Goualante du pauvre Jean*, a song steeped in the tradition of François Villon, and launched in America, was introduced to her French public for the first time. Olympia '55 also produced one of her most disturbing songs, *Légende*. With her own lyrics set to Gilbert Bécaud's music, the narrator speaks from beyond the grave about his lost love:

> Dieu n'a jamais permis
> De supprimer sa vie,
> Elle est morte pour moi,
> Et je suis mort pour elle.
> C'est en vain que j'appelle,
> Chaque nuit je l'entends pleurer
> Seule, dans son éternité.
> Christine, je t'aime!

> (God never allowed her
> To deprive herself of life,
> She died for me,
> I died for her.
> I call out for her in vain.
> Each night I hear her crying
> Alone, in her eternity.
> Christine, I love you!)

Edith returned to the Olympia in May 1956 when her *vedette-américaine* was a young Marcel Amont, who later recorded two of her songs, *Va danser* and *Les bleuets d'azur*. This time she stayed for twelve weeks and broke every attendance record – they even had to sell folding seats in the aisles. On the opening night she took twenty curtain calls. The recording of the performance sold 20,000 copies within two weeks of its release.

Her new songs included Jacques Larue's *Marie la Française*, about the French girl who becomes a prostitute in Australia; *Une dame* and *Toi qui sais* by Michel Emer; and *Soudaine une vallée*, a translation by Jean Dréjac of the American song 'Suddenly There's a Valley'. Dréjac adapted another American song, 'Black Denim Trousers and Motorcycle Boots'; it became *L'homme à la moto* and was so successful that the original version was soon forgotten. It tells the ubiquitous story of the leather-clad demon who, with his girlfriend Mary-Lou, attempts to outrace the Southern Express and fails.

Edith said at the time that she was fond of songs where someone dies at the end. It is no surprise, then, that her greatest success at Olympia '56 was *Les amants d'un jour*, arguably the best *chanson-poème* ever written.

One is immediately reminded of one of those little tourist-class hotels, sleazy, yet with a quality of their own. The woman is in the back of the café washing glasses. And . . .

> Ils sont arrivés se tenant par la main,
> L'air émerveillé de deux chérubins,
> Portant le soleil, ils ont demandés
> D'une voix tranquille,
> Un coin pour s'aimer . . .
>
> (They arrived hand in hand,
> The wondrous aura of two cherubs,
> Bringing sunshine with them.
> They asked, meekly,
> For a corner to love in . . .)

The song ends tragically, with a shattered glass dropped on the stage. The woman still washes glasses, but now her eyes are brimming with tears as she remembers,

> On les a trouvés se tenant par la main,
> Les yeux refermés, vers d'autres matins.
> Remplis de soleil, on les a couchés,
> Unis et tranquilles, dans un lit creusé . . .
>
> (They found them, hand in hand,
> Eyes closed towards other mornings.
> In the sunshine, they laid them to rest,
> Peacefully together, in a hollow bed . . .)

Ralph Harvey, an authority on the *chanson*, writing on the sleeve notes for *Lovers of Paris*, said of the song:

It is often a subject for discussion amongst critics of poetry and Piaf fans alike. Lovers for a day, described by one critic as a working-class Mayerling story with an after-taste of mysticism. It is no less a perfect union of words and music. The setting, a tawdry hotel in a Parisian slum, is in the minor key whereas the lovers themselves are in the major, their suicide providing a way of escape to love in Eternity.

Another song in a class of its own was *Le chemin des forains*, with Jean Dréjac's lyrics set to the haunting classical music of Henri Sauget, originally composed for Roland Petit's first ballet, choreographed in 1945. It was released on a hard-to-come-by Pathé-Marconi extended-play record, ESRF 1036, with the similarly classical *L'homme au piano* by Darnal, Henning and Terningsohn, and the nostalgic *Retour*, by Jean-Marie, Heyne and Masset. None of these ever wrote for Piaf again, which is a great pity because they were, and still are, way ahead of their time. Neither were they as successful as the record's title track, *C'est à Hambourg*, another favourite Piaf theme, telling of a prostitute's quest for sailors around the ports of the world. The lyrics to this song became her private property – the cover version by

Renée Lebas and a later recording by Catherine Sauvage, renowned for her interpretations of Léo Ferré, had its lyrics 'tamed down' slightly. To the English-speaking world it became an instrumental, 'On the Quayside', losing much of its effect. Edith's earlier song, *La goualante du pauvre Jean*, had suffered a similar fate in becoming 'The Poor People of Paris'.

1956 drew to a close with Edith's greatest personal triumph: Carnegie Hall in New York. It was the first time that a popular singer had performed in this, the most famous concert hall in America, a feat equalled only by Judy Garland in 1961. Fans queued for hours in sub-zero temperatures to buy tickets, many of which were snapped up by racketeers and sold on the black market for hundreds of dollars.

Carnegie Hall seated 3800 people. Such was the demand that Edith could have filled it several times over. One critic said that New York had claimed her as its own Joan of Arc. With the Americans, she could do no wrong. The Carnegie Hall performance of 13 January 1957 – an unusual date for Edith, with her superstitious nature – was taped by a fan, Stephen F. Temmer, and released on a double LP in 1977.

Edith sang twenty-seven songs, opening with *C'est pour ça*, the song she had introduced with Les Compagnons de la Chanson. Even for her, it was a difficult song and she had to struggle to meet its wide range. But if at first she sounded tremulous and slightly off-key, this was soon put right in the next song. Her heart-rending English adaptation of *Les amants d'un jour* defied even the most hard-hearted listener to remain dry-eyed. Many other songs were sung in English, including 'Autumn Leaves', 'Heaven Have Mercy' (*Miséricorde*), *La vie en rose*, the better known translation of *Hymne à l'amour* ('If You Love Me, Really Love Me'), 'The Highway' (*Un jeune homme chantait*), and 'My Lost Melody' (*Je n'en connais pas la fin*). *Monsieur Saint-Pierre* was also revived, and an American fan, Rick French, came up with an excellent translation of *Le petit homme*.

Les grognards, by Hubert Giraud and Pierre Delanoë, was given its debut at Carnegie Hall. It is a wonderful piece, opening with the marching of feet and a spoken verse: 'The Grumblers have no guns, no grenades, no shoes. They are the ghosts of Napoleon's soldiers who are haunting Paris because, in life, they never got to see it.' The song builds up in a terrific crescendo, with the rolling of drums and Piaf's voice practically raising the roof. Then it subsides and dies, leaving retreating footsteps – a masterpiece!

By now, Edith Piaf was the highest-paid female entertainer in the world. In fact, only Frank Sinatra and Bing Crosby were earning more than she was at this time. Sadly, she was forced to admit to herself that her marriage was over. In *Ma vie* she tells the story.

I made him swear never to remove his wedding ring. We were shooting a film at Vichy and his dresser came in, reminding him to take off his ring. He had broken his vow. I closed my eyes to hide the tears. We were heading towards catastrophe. Two months later we were divorced.

The couple were formally divorced on 15 May 1957. It would be wrong, however, to assume that their union had been a complete failure. Certainly, Edith would never be able to offer her love to one man alone; her public *had* to come first. Without Pills's help, it is doubtful she would have pulled through her drink and drug ordeal as well as she did – if indeed at all.

Even so, some of the scars inflicted during those four tortured years would never heal.

9

The Great Piaf!

Carnegie Hall was the turning-point in Edith's career. In America as well as in France, she had become a living legend. A 'sacred monster'. Even the Soviet Union, which had no chance of ever seeing her, thought there was no one like her. Australia, New Zealand and Great Britain made offers that no one in their right mind could have refused. Canada was the only English-speaking country, apart from America, that apparently interested her, however, and even then she preferred the largely French-speaking provinces. So, why this reluctance? Australasia was too far away to risk. The British, she declared, had never understood her, although she almost accepted an offer to sing there in 1962, by which time, of course, she was too ill to travel far.

And after Carnegie Hall?

In California the Texan millionaire Ted Morrow booked El Mocambo, one of the state's most exclusive (and expensive) night-clubs for what he predicted would be the 'party of the century'. Depositing $45,000 with the management, he asked them to engage the best female artiste they could think of. They chose Edith. After a knock-out performance the film mogul, Darryl Zanuck, rushed over to her table and offered her a vast sum for the film rights to her life story.

Politely, he was turned down.

The Americans adored her, and affectionately christened her 'Miss Courage'. She in turn loved and respected them. Of course, because their morals were considered to be higher than those of the Europeans, she had to be on her best behaviour. No drugs, no getting drunk – a far cry from the America of today.

In those days, the United States probably had just one singer of equal intensity, Jane Froman. She was a highly emotive performer who was crippled during World War II in a plane crash near Lisbon. The world followed her fight back to health, and her story was told in the film of 1952, *With a Song in My Heart*, starring Susan Hayward, and using Froman's singing voice. Was Zanuck planning a similarly 'Hollywoodised' account of Piaf's life?

The American tour lasted almost a year. Edith had tremendous successes in Las Vegas and Chicago. In San Francisco the captain of the French battleship *Jeanne d'Arc* invited her aboard his vessel to review the French Navy. Edith adored men in uniform. The students of New York's Columbia University had little difficulty in persuading her to sing *L'accordéoniste* on New Year's Day 1957, whilst standing under the Statue of Liberty, muffled against the freezing cold.

Edith also toured South America, with engagements in Rio de Janeiro, Buenos Aires and Peru. Here she heard the young Spanish singer, Carmella, singing her latest hit. Edith 'borrowed' the music, and asked her friend Michel Rivgauche to supply her with a suitable lyric. As with *L'homme à la moto*, the song would soon be forgotten in its original form. It became *La foule*.

La foule tells the story of a holiday crowd: a bewildered girl is suddenly swept into the arms of a young man by the ebb and flow of the dancers in the street. For a few moments she has found true happiness! But her joy is short-lived as the same crowd tears them apart, never to meet again. One is reminded of that famous closing scene in Marcel Carné's masterpiece of the cinema, *Les enfants du paradis*, when the luckless mime, Baptiste, loses his beloved Garance to the hustle and bustle of the carnival crowd.

> Effrénée par la foule
> Qui s'élance, et qui danse
> Une folle parandôle,
> Je suis emportée au loin . . .

> (Frantic with the crowd
> Springing forwards,
> Dancing a crazy parandole,
> I was carried far away . . .)

The same session at which this was recorded, 25 November 1957, produced no fewer than five Piaf classics. *Les grognards* has already been mentioned. *Les prisons du roi*, another of the handful of her songs not written especially for her, had been translated from the original 'Allentown Jail' by Michel Rivgauche again. He was an eccentric-looking character with a little moustache, untidy hair and long, thin eyebrows – Edith had once described him as 'looking like the bad guy in a silent movie'. His translation stuck pretty close to the American song: the woman's lover has been thrown into the king's prison because he has stolen jewels for her. Now, she begs the king to put her in prison with him because she has stolen his heart. A somewhat schmaltzy, over-sentimental ballad had been transformed into a *chanson-dramatique*, complete with choir. *Salle d'attente*, with another lyric by Michel Rivgauche, set to an alarmingly difficult composition by Marguerite Monnot, was sung with comparative ease by Edith, whose range had seemingly doubled overnight.

The final song from the session was *Opinion publique*, lyrically one of her most interesting works. It is almost a *chanson-parlée*: rumour follows the man everywhere, in the street, in the cafés. His reputation is advertised in the town hall and the market place – until one Sunday, standing in the square he cries, 'It isn't true!' He is a famous man, now, but the rumours are the same . . .

> On dit qu'il a, on dit qu'il est,
> On dit qu'il a fait,
> A fait ceci, a fait cela,
> Non, il a dit ça? Oui, il a dit ça!

> (They say he's got, they say he is,
> They say he's done,
> He's done this, he's done that,
> No, he said that? Yes, he said that!)

Edith's lengthy spell in the United States made her homesick for France. She wasn't interested in sightseeing. Niagara Falls she dismissed as 'just a lot of water'. Her

favourite country air was that of a park in Paris; her
favourite mountain, Montmartre. As an *enfant du faubourg*
the artificial glamour of Hollywood bored her.

During Edith's absence Marguerite Monnot had collaborated with the singer Colette Renard. Between them they
had produced the highly successful stage musical, *Irma la
Douce*. Whilst apart the two friends had kept in touch by
link-up or telephone; it is estimated that a third of Edith's
earnings went on telephone calls alone. Now, she was
welcomed at Orly like a queen.

At the Boulevard Lannes life resumed its usual hectic
pace. But Edith's health had begun to fail. The joints in
her hands were knotted through rheumatism; she was ill
far too often. But her philosophy of life was the same
in 1957 as it was a few years later when, extremely
sick, she was interviewed by a very daring Paul Gianoli
of Radio Luxembourg. Her replies to his questions were
candid:

GIANOLI: Edith Piaf, are you afraid of dying?

PIAF: I'm not afraid of death. I don't think I've ever
harmed anyone, so I don't fear chastisement.
If you act with sincerity, you haven't much to
fear when you present yourself to the Great
Judge.

GIANOLI: You've had many lovers. Have there been as
many deceptions?

PIAF: I've never been deceived. The ones that
I loved brought me a great experience. I
regret · nothing I've done or known. If I
could, I'd begin again. I thank heaven for
giving me this life – I've lived life to the
full!

GIANOLI: 'I don't like unhappiness!' You repeat this
line in Prevert's song. Are you expressing
your own opinion?

PIAF: Yes. Jacques Prevert understood all that I feel, and that's a fact. His song is a description of my almost permanent spiritual state.

GIANOLI: The doctors who care for you. Are you aware how you baffle them?

PIAF: Oh, yes! I baffle them. They don't expect my reactions. At the very moment they think I'm done for, I pull through. When they think they have saved me, I fail! They're getting used to me now!

GIANOLI: You do acknowledge the fact that you're not following a very reasonable life style?

PIAF: It isn't a question of regime. My illness is due to fatigue and car accidents. I've always begun working again, because my public has been waiting for me.

GIANOLI: At the clinic, the last time, did you have the feeling that it was very serious?

PIAF: I honestly believed that I wouldn't come out. I was even waiting for the end. For a few days I thought it was all over, without sadness. I'd made up my mind. 'This is it,' I told myself. 'So what? Surely, it must be good over on the other side!'

By the end of 1957 rehearsals were well under way for Olympia '58. Marguerite Monnot, Michel Rivgauche and Pierre Delanoë had been commissioned to write a set of new songs. And before the opening night, there would be the customary tour of the provinces.

Louis Barrier had provided her with a new *vedette-américaine*, a young singer called Félix Marten.

Marten was talented, and according to the people who were working with him at the time, he knew it. For Edith, his fine singing voice and macho appeal more than compensated for his almighty ego. His songs, however, did not appeal to her. *Fais-moi un cheque* and *T'as une belle cravate* were not love songs, she declared, and Marten's delivery was very wooden, and unsuited to his good looks.

She decided to remodel him.

As was expected, they became lovers.

In the middle of the tour Edith telephoned the Monnot-Contet-Rivgauche team and at a moment's notice commanded them to drop everything and meet her at Nevers, her next stop on the road. They obeyed – how could they possibly refuse? – and for the next forty-eight hours the team worked without a break. Their *coup* paid off. Marten had his new repertoire, though there would only be the one big hit, *Je t'aime mon amour*.

Between her tour and Olympia '58, Edith shot her fourth and final feature film, *Les amants de demain*. It was a superb film, scripted by that other 'sacred monster' of the French cinema, Pierre Brasseur, and again directed by her friend, Marcel Blistène. It boasted a fine supporting cast, headed by the much-acclaimed Mona Goya (it would be her last film), Raymond Souplex, Armand Mestral, and another friend and one-time songwriter, the comedian Francis Blanche.

The story could have been the setting for one of Edith's songs. Like *Neuf garçons et un cœur*, it begins one Christmas Eve, though the story here is a far cry from fantasy. Pierre, a composer, is on the run from the police after murdering his wife. When his car breaks down he seeks shelter at Les Géraniums, a provincial hotel-restaurant. Here, he is thrown headlong into an even more dreadful situation when he meets the hotel owner (Armand Mestral) and his wife, Simone (Piaf). The husband is an unfaithful thug who cheats on his wife and beats her, subsequently driving her to drink. Pierre stays the night. He and Simone fall in love. The husband finds out and tries to kill Pierre, only to be killed himself by his miserable wife. The film ends with Simone and her lover, having fulfilled their destiny, descending the stairs to the waiting police van, accompanied by Piaf's voice singing the title song.

The soundtrack for the film was composed by Marguerite Monnot. *Tant qu'il y aura des jours* and the haunting *Fais comme si* had lyrics by Michel Rivgauche. Henri Contet wrote the stirring title track, and the sublime *Les neiges de Finlande*, the shortest of all the Piaf songs, and surely one of the most poignant lullabies of all time:

> Le Méchant Loup est un archange,
> Les ogres mangent des oranges,
> Cendrillon file la laine,
> Pour habiller Croque-mitaine,
> Et je le crois!
> Alors je dors sur des légendes,
> Et je peux voir dans mon grenier,
> Tomber les neiges de Finlande!
>
> (The Big Bad Wolf is an archangel,
> Ogres eat oranges,
> Cinderella spins wool
> To clothe the Bogey Man,
> And I believe it!
> I sleep upon legends,
> And in my loft I can see
> The falling snows of Finland!)

This song, more than any other, defines Edith's childlike belief in fairy-stories, and the fact that all will turn out well in the end. In spite of her experiences she was still incredibly naive, sometimes, when it came to assessing her future. In some of her more sentimental songs, such as *La chanson bleue* and *Le ciel est fermé*, this naivity is especially poignant. For the sleeve notes of the elusive soundtrack record of *Les amants de demain* (Pathé-Marconi ESRF 1198) Marcel Blistène wrote:

> 'The Snows of Finland' reveals a new facet of
> Piaf's talent. It is a lullaby where she is
> wholly sweetness, wholly tenderness, with an
> infinite fragility.

Not content with writing the script for the film, Pierre Brasseur also collaborated on a song with Michel Emer – one of the rare occasions when he did not supply words *and* music. With Edith in mind Brasseur asked the eminent playwright Jean Anouilh for permission to quote a line from his celebrated play, *La sauvage*. Naturally, this was granted and the song was *Et pourtant*:

> Et pourtant,
> Il y aura toujours un pauvre chien perdu,
> Quelque part,
> Qui m'empêchera d'être heureuse!

> (Nevertheless,
> There will always be a poor lost dog,
> Somewhere,
> Which prevents me from being happy!)

Edith's new season at the Olympia opened on 17 February 1958, and ran for four months. Astonishingly, she broke all her previous records, both in attendance and box office takings. The drink-drug era may have taken a severe toll on her health, but her voice and stage-presence were more powerful than ever. Her subject range was wide, too, from Marguerite Monnot's *Comme moi*, to the unusually gay and lively *Mon manège à moi*.

> Tu me fais tourner la tête,
> Mon manège à moi, c'est toi!
> Je suis toujours à la fête,
> Quand tu me prends dans tes bras!

> (You set my head reeling,
> You're my very own merry-go-round!
> I'm always at the fair,
> When you take me in your arms!)

On the personal side, Félix Marten was an unexpected failure. Arrogant, cynical, and too sure of himself, he fell out with Edith half-way through the Olympia season.

Her friends were stunned. Marten had become one of 'Piaf's Boys'. He had even collaborated with Jean-Pierre Moulin on a song, *Je me souviens d'une chanson*. He had been the first man after her four 'dangerous years'. Her friends were concerned for her welfare; she had fought her way back to the top, and she was alone again.

Her first autobiography, *Au bal de la chance*, was published in 1958. Edith chose the title, inspired by the song of the same name which had been written by Jacques Larue and Norbert Glanzberg, and recorded in 1952. Though 'The Wheel of Fortune' (as it became in the English translation) lacked the stark controversy of her posthumously published memoirs, it did verge on philosophy – she knew what she was writing about because she had been there. Her friend Jean Cocteau penned the introduction:

When I say that Madame Edith Piaf has genius, I am borrowing from Stendhal. She is unique – there has never been another like her, and there never will be! Like Yvette Guilbert and Yvonne George, like Rachel or Réjane, she burns brightly in the nocturnal solitude of the skies of France.

Of the Piaf voice and performance, he says:

Have you heard the nightingale? She toils. She hesitates. She rasps. She chokes. She rises and falls. Then suddenly she sings, she astonishes! Edith Piaf, like the invisible nightingale, installed on her branch, becomes herself invisible. Nothing is left of her save her eyes, her pale hands, her waxen forehead reflecting the light, and that voice which swells, which mounts, which little by little replaces her. The soul of the street filters into every room of the town. It is no longer Madame Edith Piaf that sings. It is the rain that falls, the wind that blows, the moonlight that spreads its mantle of light!

Au bal de la chance ended with the phrase: 'better to live than vegetate'. Edith had adopted it from someone else who had fought constantly against bouts of ill-health: her friend, President Eisenhower. The phrase could easily have been her own, especially when it came to getting over Félix Marten. Within days of their break-up he had been replaced by a handsome young man who, as far as her career was concerned, would be the most important lover since Henri Contet.

Georges Moustaki was a budding singer-songwriter who was then appearing at the College Inn in Montparnasse. He was a Greek – Edith's second one. Before going on stage himself, he always made a point of going to see Edith's show at the Olympia. He was a friend of her guitarist, Henri Crolla, a cousin of the gypsy guitarist, Django Reinhardt, and composer of two songs, *Cri de cœur* and *Tatave*. He arranged a meeting in Edith's dressing room.

Moustaki has never disclosed their subsequent conversation. Needless to say, that very evening Edith accompanied him to the College Inn, 'in his battered old wreck of a car'. Within a week he had moved into the boulevard Lannes.

Moustaki had more in common with Piaf than most of the others. He preferred to live each day as it came. He enjoyed the all-night revelries, and did not mind slaving over one song for hours, or even days, on end. He comfortably tolerated the snatched meals because, he claimed, he was a gypsy at heart. He withstood Edith's fiery temper whenever things were not going her way, which was often. It is said that within the Piaf household there was usually more war than peace, and that they fought like cat and dog. According to close sources, Edith loved a brawl and never cared for her current man until he had slapped her. Several photographs taken at the time show her wearing heavy make-up to camouflage her bruises. And yet by all accounts she was happier in 1958 than she had been for some time.

Moustaki became her personal guitarist. She shortened his name to Jo. Louis Barrier was planning her next trip to the United States and she had been booked for a four-week stint at the Waldorf Astoria in New York. Her departure was scheduled for 18 September 1958, and she had decided to take her latest discovery with her.

At once, Moustaki set about writing her some new songs. His ideas were fresh, and as diverse as his talent: the romantic 'Eden Blues'; the nostalgic simplicity of *Les orgues de barbarie*; *L'étranger*, based on Moustaki's experiences as an immigrant; and the song which some critics have described as a thinly disguised account of his attitude towards Edith – the tense, passionate *Le gitan et la fille*.

> Le gitan a dit à la fille,
> 'Qu'importe le prix de l'amour?
> Pour toi j'irai finir mes jours
> Derrière les grilles.
> J'irai tuer ceux qui te regardent!'
>
> (The gypsy said to the girl,
> 'No matter the price of love,
> For you I'll end my days
> Behind bars.
> I'll kill any man that looks at you!')

After the Olympia Edith and Moustaki toured France. He was, at twenty-four, eighteen years her junior. She showered him with gifts – she bought him a platinum cigarette lighter, and when he lost it she bought him another. He became a 'Piaf Boy'; like all his predecessors, he would go far, solely because of her.

Edith's hectic schedule had sapped her strength, however, and her doctors advised her to spend some time resting in the country before embarking on the American tour. She rented a house at Condé-sur-Vesgre, in the Seine-et-Oise department, and gathered her entourage about her. One of these was Marcel Cerdan Junior: since the champion's death she had become self-appointed godmother to his sons, and young Marcel was her favourite. Many years later he portrayed his own father in the film *Edith et Marcel*, a somewhat glossy account of what some had called 'the love affair of the century'.

On 7 September Marcel was due to fly home to his family in Casablanca. Edith decided to accompany him to Orly airport. Moustaki was driving her DS19 and she was sitting beside him. Marcel and his girlfriend were sitting in the back. It was raining heavily. The car skidded suddenly, and somersaulted off the road. Moustaki and the girl were unhurt. Marcel suffered cuts and bruises. Edith was less fortunate. When the ambulance arrived she was stretched out at the side of the road, clutching Marlene Dietrich's cross with its seven emeralds. She was taken to the hospital at Rambouillet with a four-inch gash above her forehead, a split lip, severed tendons in her left hand, and severe facial abrasions. The car, a total write-off, was towed into a garage near Dreux – indeed, when one looks at pictures of the wreckage, one is amazed that anyone could have been pulled out of the car alive.

Most of her injuries were patched up, though the doctors were worried that the gash across her forehead would leave a scar – unthinkable, under stage lights, and with the American tour imminent. Edith was not bothered about this. She was more concerned over her split lip, for this impeded her speech and made singing practically impossible.

Louis Barrier advised her to cancel the tour. It was not a wise thing to do. There had been difficulties before, she declared, which she had always overcome. Singing was her whole life. She could let herself down – her public never! During the next few weeks she subjected herself to a series of agonising facial massages. Gradually, the scars were smoothed away.

Edith arrived in America a month late, but to an ecstatic reception. But if the Piaf voice was in fine fettle – and indeed, after each relapse in her health it only seemed to increase in its power and depth of feeling – the Piaf body was not. She opened at the Waldorf Astoria. On 20 February 1959, she collapsed on stage. In the wings she vomited blood. She was rushed to the Presbyterian Hospital on 168th Street. The surgeons had to fight to save her life, and she only just managed to pull through. A perforated stomach ulcer was diagnosed; during the four-hour operation she was given several blood transfusions. For a week hospital bulletins described her condition as critical.

The Americans were stunned. They had thought her invincible, and with the shadow of death looming over her they sent so many flowers that they overflowed into the corridor outside her room. The hospital switchboard was jammed by calls from well-wishers and fans, the most faithful of whom kept all-night vigils outside in the street, praying and humming her songs.

When Edith came to after her operation, Moustaki was no longer there. She refers to the incident in *Ma vie*, and whilst not actually mentioning him by name, it is obviously Moustaki about whom she says:

> I asked my clairvoyant if he had seen anything. He told me categorically, 'The man in your life. You must leave him or he will make you unhappy.' So I looked at my lover – in spite of his velvet gaze and tenderness he was a hard, cynical, dislikeable boy. When I went into the hospital, I asked him if he loved me. He replied, 'F------ leave me alone. We're finished.' I called him every single day after the operation. He had left me to amuse himself in Florida. He told me, sarcastically, 'The sun is shining, here. I'm in excellent health. There are *girls* here!'

Moustaki had replaced Félix Marten overnight. Now he received similar treatment. If Edith had intended keeping him hanging on until she had found a suitable replacement, her illness had broken her regular pattern, and she had been prevented from doing so. Now there was someone else, as far from her world as any man could be. He was a young American painter called Douglas Davis. And like Claude Figus, he was a 'groupie'.

Dreaming of holding an exhibition of his work in New York, Douglas had gone to see Edith at the Waldorf Astoria, hoping to meet her and pluck up enough courage to ask her to sit for him. He had probably been in the audience when she collapsed. During her illness, rather than buy her huge bouquets or baskets of flowers, he had bought her simple bunches of violets, knowing nothing about her superstitions and foibles! This, and the fact that he spent two hours every day on the New York subway bringing them to her, touched Edith's heart. Twenty-three years before, at Gerny's, the aviator Jean Mermoz had been the first man ever to give her flowers – violets.

Louis Barrier arranged an introduction. For Edith, it was love at first sight even though Douggie, as she baptised him, was twenty-three years her junior. It was just as well that she spoke English because Douggie hardly knew a word of French. Needless to say, he got what he had wanted. Edith sat for him.

On 25 March 1959, a few days after her discharge from the Presbyterian Hospital, Edith collapsed again and suffered a relapse. There followed a second major operation. This time when she came to, she was not alone. Her new lover was holding her hand. And when she looked up she saw five gaily-coloured balloons attached to the ceiling. Douglas had brought them on the subway! Luckily, there was a photographer on hand to record the happy event: the result is most touching.

Two months later she left the hospital, clutching Douglas Davis' hand. She had lost weight, and looked gaunt. But for Piaf, the show had to go on. She had been booked to appear on the Ed Sullivan Show, to be followed by a week-long stint in Washington – and a ten-day tour of Canada. According to Mômone, during Edith's first operation the doctors had discovered cancer, too late to effect a cure. True or not, the great singer was almost dying.

She was faced with an enormous hospital bill. Robert Chauvigny, her musical director, and her musicians had spent a frugal winter in New York, taking whatever work came their way, and living on next to nothing most of the time. Needless to say, not one of them had even thought of deserting her. Edith was broke, but if Louis Barrier contemplated cancelling her forthcoming engagements, he knew that he would only be wasting his time.

Edith returned to the Waldorf Astoria and bravely carried on where she had left off. The American public had been good to her. She wanted to leave them with happy memories, for she knew in her heart of hearts that she would never see them again.

10

'I Regret Nothing!'

Edith had left Paris with one man. When she arrived at Orly on 21 June 1959 it was on the arm of another – Douglas Davis. Newsreel pictures show her smiling radiantly, in fact there are few photographs and films of her from this time when she is not smiling or looking happy. In spite of the drama and intensity of her songs, like Damia and Fréhel before her, she was not a morbid woman – far from it! Life had to be lived to the full, or not at all. In an article for *Paris Match*, celebrating the twentieth anniversary of her death in 1983, Alexandre Astrue said, unfairly, that she had only searched for happiness within her songs. This is not true, as many of her surviving friends have confirmed. The actress Catherine Jan, also a well-known street organist and clairvoyant, attending a showing of a new print of the film *Neuf garçons et un cœur* in Paris in 1974 told the author that 'the Piaf laugh could demolish a building at 200 metres'. Madame Jan, appeared in *Les amants de domain* and remained a good friend.

Michel Emer and Marc Bonel, her accordionist, added similar anecdotes.

In Paris, suddenly propelled into the melée that was the boulevard Lannes, Douglas Davis was decidedly out of his depth. He was an artist; he was in the cultural centre of his world; Paris was waiting to be explored and committed to canvas; there were galleries galore, and museums. Typically tyrannical, Edith refused to let him out of her sight for a moment. She also had the habit of having the central heating on, full-blast, which in June must have been distressing.

She did, however, allow him to open his paint-box, and the portraits which he did of her are striking, depicting a Piaf hitherto unseen by the media. Mômone described them as 'the Piaf that the people carry around in their hearts'. Three

117

achieved world fame on record covers: who has not been moved, studying these whilst thrilling to the Piaf voice?

During Edith's absence, manuscripts had piled up. In America she had rehearsed *Milord*, Georges Moustaki's last song before he deserted her. Marguerite Monnot and her entourage had sung it to her, when she landed at Orly. For the moment, she put this one aside. She would never forgive Moustaki, even though they remained friends for the rest of her life. Contracts had poured in, and she had every intention of fulfilling them all. She began rehearsals for a forthcoming tour of France, ignoring the pleas of her doctors and friends, who feared a relapse, and even death itself.

In July 1959 she paid another visit to her clairvoyant. He told her, 'You are going through a period of well-being at the moment, but in a few months there will be long months of suffering. I have never seen death as close to you as I do now.'

Because Douglas disliked driving French cars, she bought him an expensive Chevrolet. He was driving it on the first day of her tour when it shot off the road and hit a crash barrier. Douglas was unhurt. Michel Rivgauche, travelling in the back, was badly bruised. Edith had three broken ribs.

There was no question of cancelling the tour. Edith was put into a tight cast and given morphine. This time it was for her own good, and she did not become addicted. Her doctor watched her from the wings. Singing caused her so much pain that she had to fake curtain calls in order to leave the stage for more injections. She was also taking cortisone for her rheumatism, which made her face bloated. On stage the audiences saw a pathetic little Piaf doll in a black dress, her make-up smudged and her stockings creased. Only the voice had changed for the better.

Edith and Douglas spent a short time in Cannes. Here he became her swimming instructor. Edith, who had always avoided the sun, could now be seen sunning herself on the beach, an old-fashioned swimsuit covering her bandages. Cannes, of course, had offered Douglas a once-in-a-lifetime opportunity to meet his idol, Picasso. He also visited those localities associated with Van Gogh and Cézanne – against Edith's will, of course, which led to inevitable rows.

By the time they reached Bordeaux, the young painter had decided that he had had enough. He walked out on her in the middle of the night. Edith ran after him, a coat thrown over her nightdress. As she arrived at the railway station, the train was pulling out. Once again she was alone. Two years later the theme was used for one of her more philosophical songs, *C'est peut-être ça*.

With the exception of a poor tape recording of *Faut-pas qu'il se figure*, made in January 1959 and subsequently dropped, Edith only entered the recording studio once that year. This was on 5 August when she recorded Moustaki's *T'es beau tu sais* and her only British chart success, *Milord*:

> Allez, venez, Milord,
> Vous asseoir à ma table!
> Il fait si froid, dehors,
> Ici, c'est confortable!
>
> (Come on, Milord,
> Sit at my table!
> It's so cold outside,
> Here, it's comfortable!)

Milord tells the story of a prostitute – not an uncommon theme – who works the dockland beat. She meets an elegant gentleman with a long, flowing silk scarf; she has seen him the day before, on the arm of a beautiful girl. Now she understands how sad he feels, for his sweetheart's ship has sailed away. She tells him,

> L'amour ça fait pleurer,
> Comme quoi l'existence.
> Ça vous donne toutes les chances,
> Pour les reprendre après!
>
> (Love makes you cry,
> Life's like that.
> It gives you all the opportunities,
> Only to snatch them back again!)

The song was translated into English by Bunny Lewis, an impresario who once again invited her to visit Britain, without success. Britain, she said, would be like conquering America all over again. Besides which, by the autumn of 1959 she was far too ill to take on too many new challenges.

After her successful French tour and disastrous love affair, Edith left for Sweden. An earlier tour of this country had left her feeling so homesick that she had chartered a DC9 to take her and an entourage of seven back to Paris for a single meal – extravagant, even by her standards. She fared little better this time. Louis Barrier had secured her a booking at the Stockholm Bernsbee, then the country's most prestigious music-hall. She was singing *Mon manège à moi* before an audience of 5000 when she collapsed.

This time she really thought that she was going to die, and what terrified her most of all was not death itself, but the fact that she was going to die in a foreign country. She was flown straight to the American Hospital at Neuilly, where surgeons performed an emergency operation for pancreatitis. She almost died on the operating table, and after her discharge Louis Barrier took her to his house at Richebourg where she slowly recuperated, accompanied only by her nurse and the ever-present Claude Figus.

Edith was now suffering from acute agoraphobia. She was so crippled with rheumatism that she was unable to walk unaided. Her doctor prescribed her the best, most expensive chiropractor in France. His name was Lucien Vaimber, and later she sang a song about him. She suffered excruciating pain as Vaimber unknotted her joints and spine. She recovered, only to relapse into a hepatic coma.

Incredibly, by 13 May 1960 she was back in the Pathé-Marconi studio, working on her forthcoming album, *Huit chansons nouvelles*. By 20 May the album was ready for release. Such was her degree of professionalism that all the songs were recorded with the one take, and the album was an innovation. Two of the numbers, *T'es beau tu sais* and *Opinion publique* had already been recorded, and *Cri de cœur* has already been mentioned. *C'est l'amour* was a Piaf-Monnot creation which may be described as Edith's credo – that true love can only be bought with tears. The other songs were all new works by young composers. Claude Leveillé, a young Canadian for whom Edith had much respect and few tantrums, collaborated with Henri Contet on *Le vieux piano*, and with Michel Rivgauche on *Ouragan*, a truly inspired song in which Edith's voice really does lash out like a hurricane. Julien Bouget wrote the moving testimony, *Je suis à toi*, and Robert Gall and Florence Véran were responsible for *Les amants merveilleux*.

On 27 May she recorded one of her most ingenious songs, *Boulevard du crime*, in every sense a symphony *en miniature* by Claude Leveillé. This was released in Britain on the *C'est la Piaf* album in 1961, but until recently has been elusive to Piaf's French admirers.

These recording sessions behind her, Edith began rehearsing for a new tour of the provinces, to be followed by a season at the Olympia. It was sheer madness. Her friends begged her not to do it, but she ploughed on relentlessly, knowing only too well that she was killing herself.

Then, a miracle!

In the summer of 1960 Michel Vaucaire, a composer friend, introduced her to a young man called Charles Dumont.

Dumont, at thirty-one, had already contributed to the *chanson*, writing songs for performers as diverse as Luis Mariano, Tino Rossi, and Sacha Distel. He had approached Edith several times through mutual acquaintances, but for some reason she had always refused to have anything to do with him. It is even suggested that she may have disliked him. Even now, when Michel Vaucaire pleaded with her to see him, she did so reluctantly.

Feeling decidedly ill at ease, Dumont sat at Edith's piano and played the music he had composed to accompany Michel Vaucaire's simple, but effective lyric:

> Non, rien de rien!
> Non je ne regrette rien!
> Ni le bien qu'on m'a fait,
> Ni le mal!
> Tout ça m'est bien égal!

(Nothing!
I regret nothing!
Neither the good done to me,
Nor the bad!
It's all the same to me!)

The rest, of course, is part of the legend. If someone has only heard one Piaf song, it would be this one. *Non je ne regrette rien* became Edith's greatest hit in France and abroad, and will always be identified with her. As far as its composers were concerned, they never looked back. Dumont also became Edith's chief composer, replacing even the stalwart Marguerite Monnot. In all he wrote the music for more than thirty of her songs, almost all of them million-sellers.

Edith's 'suicide tour', as it became known, began on 14 October 1960 and opened at Rheims, where *Non je ne regrette rien* proved so popular that she had to perform it several times. But the tour robbed her of what little strength she had left. For eight weeks she fed on a diet of pep-pills, steadfastly refusing the needle, even though for once in her life it would have done her good.

Some establishments were so afraid of her dying on them that they cruelly cancelled her contracts, though Edith later admitted that she was so ill and confused that she never knew what was happening at the time, otherwise they might not have got away with it so easily. She also claimed that she even had to read the posters outside the theatres to identify which town she was singing in.

At Mauberge, the audience were informed, minutes before her performance was due to start, that she was too sick to sing. Edith, waiting in the wings when the announcement was given out, refused to be beaten. When Robert Chauvigny told her that he would not direct the orchestra, she seized the baton and threatened to direct herself. This would have proved inordinately difficult, of course, and for more than the obvious reason – during the later Piaf performances the orchestra was rarely seen because it was hidden behind a curtain, which really goes to show just how perfect her timing was. She hardly ever missed a cue or made a mistake.

At Nancy and Chaumont she sang with a raging fever and had to be carried on and off the stage. On 19 December – it was her forty-fifth birthday – she sang at Thionville to what can only be described as mass hysteria. This spurred her on, but later, at Cameo in Béthune, she was obliged to stop half-way through her first song, *Le ballet des cœurs*, short of breath. After a drink of water, she continued. The show was transmitted live on French radio, and millions of listeners had tuned in. The radio commentator, Claude Lableau, observed – as did many – that it was astonishing how she could manipulate her crippled hands only on stage.

Edith managed to complete her performance that night, but she was absolutely worn out when Lableau interviewed her. His questions were representative of those of the whole of France – and beyond:

LABLEAU: Madame, many people ask the question: why, in spite of your illness, do you keep on singing?

PIAF: It is an accidental illness, nothing to do with my general state of health, which is quite good.

LABLEAU: You would like to reassure our listeners of *that*?

PIAF: I am very well. I really want to sing. I've never needed to sing as much as I do now – it's necessary for my health.

LABLEAU: Don't you feel *tired*?

PIAF: Absolutely not! Singing isn't weariness and hard work. It's a pleasure!

The tour ended with a recital at Dreux, which must have brought back memories of her appalling car crash, and the photographs taken during this performance are both alarming and heart-breaking. The theatre manager, seeing the state she was in, would not even consider letting her go on stage.

Louis Barrier and Charles Dumont had carried her from her dressing room to the wings. Her one wish, she declared, was to die on stage with the applause still ringing in her ears. No one tried to stop her then. When the curtain opened she was leaning against the piano, unable to move. She shouted to her hysterical audience, 'I love you! You're my life! Please, let me sing!' There was hardly a dry eye in the house. But after the seventh song she collapsed and was unable to get up. The curtain closed slowly . . . The people filed out in silence, and many believed that she really had died – and no one asked for their money back. Bruno Coquatrix and Louis Barrier took her to the clinic at Meudon.

It was literally days from the Olympia première, and still she refused to accept defeat. During the tour she had recorded more prolifically than at any other time in her career: twelve songs. With the exception of three, all were by Dumont. *La vie l'amour* was a short, lively but noisy piece composed by her musical director, Robert Chauvigny. *Je m'imagine* was the last but one song to come from the pen of Marguerite Monnot. It was not released in France until after her death; in England it was released on a charity record, and sold well. Hurt by Edith's growing habit of substituting Dumont's songs for hers, Marguerite had been noticeably absent from the tour. She was, in fact, ill herself, though Edith had not been told. *Jérusalem* was by Robert Chabrier and Jo Moutet, not two of her regular composers. It featured a most unusual un-Piaf-like Yiddish chant, the recurrent religious theme – in this case, Jesus himself – and though it is not one of her best-known songs, it should be.

But if Edith was fascinated by Dumont the composer, she was not over-keen on the man himself. There was always a certain amount of distance between them, even though at this point in their respective careers they were practically never apart. With no man in her life, Edith was more ruthless than usual. For several months Dumont saw little of his wife and two daughters, and Edith obviously suspected that he might have had something to hide in that respect. Dumont's rewards, though, were more than adequate.

The seventeen new songs expected to be included in the Olympia programme had been well aired in the provinces, and *Non je ne regrette rien* was proving the biggest hit of the year in France. Edith was, of course, still very sick. She broadcast a personal message to her fans on French radio, telling them that she was looking forward to seeing them, thus ending any speculation that she might pull out at the last moment, especially as, half-way through rehearsals, Robert Chauvigny himself became gravely ill and had to be replaced by the younger, fitter Jacques Lesage.

Lesage and Edith had first met in 1959, when he had been director to Felix Marten. For Lesage, working with Piaf was a monstrous ordeal, as Jean Noli points out in his moving biography of Edith's last years, *Edith Piaf: trois ans pour mourir*.

Jacques Lesage was a pitiful sight to see. At first he had appeared hale and hearty, solid as a bank. By the end of the month he had the transfixed expression of a Christian martyr. Like the rest of us he wore the stigmata common to the prisoners of the boulevard Lannes – ashen complexion, rings around his eyes, bitter taste in his mouth, joyless smile, vague, dimwitted . . .

Monique Lange, in her *Histoire de Piaf*, states that Piaf had decided to save the Olympia in the same way that Joan of Arc had decided to save France. There is no better way of describing her own resurrection, and that of the famous music-hall's director, Bruno Coquatrix. Coquatrix had serious heart trouble. He was also in debt to the tune of fifty million *anciens francs*. He had begged Edith to sing at the Olympia, knowing that only she was capable of filling the auditorium night after night, thus putting both their heads above water again. It must be said, however, that for Edith, who was almost constantly in debt, financial reward did not figure very highly on her list of priorities. She sang because it was in her blood. She sang because she had to. Otherwise, life would have been meaningless. When asked once what she would do if she *had* to stop singing, she replied, 'I'd make films!' She was not being serious, of course. The fact that she might die at any moment did not frighten her; the fact that she might be unable to sing on any particular night did.

Before the Olympia première there were two significant events. First, she appeared with Charles Dumont on the popular television show *Cinq Colonnes à la Une*, hosted by Pierre Desgraupes. Now the French people could see for themselves that she was in a fit state to sing. She and Dumont sang their own composition, *Les amants*. Later, he expressed his dislike of the song and even branded it as an amateur production – Edith's voice had only been used in the background of the recording, chanting and echoing parts of the refrain. But the song, released on a French EP with two other songs under the title *Edith Piaf et Charles Dumont chantent l'amour* sold a quarter of a million copies within a week of its release.

Secondly, whilst Edith was in the middle of her final rehearsal for the Olympia – at a cinema near Versailles on Christmas Day, no less – a telegram arrived from Marlene Dietrich: 'IMPOSSIBLE TO COME AND APPLAUD YOU. GOOD LUCK AND GOOD HEALTH. I KISS YOU. MARLENE.'

This dispelled any suggestion that her friend had deserted her in her hour of need, unable to tolerate any longer her abuse of alcohol and drugs. Now, the show could go on!

As Catherine Jan explains, on the eve of the première the boulevard Lannes was like a mad-house. Well-wishers filed in and out all day. Edith's new black dress and shoes arrived, but she changed her mind at the last minute, deciding to wear an old pair of slip-ons and a dress which she had been singing in for years.

Bruno Coquatrix had signed her up for four weeks, with as many extensions as she wanted, such was his confidence in her abilities. The possibility of a relapse must have been at the back of his mind, however. The première had initially been set for mid-January, but because she was in such good form, it was brought forward by several weeks. This presented her with some difficulties. Some of the songs – *Mon vieux Lucien* in particular – had not been rehearsed sufficiently. In fact, the night of 29 December 1960 should have been little more than a rehearsal in itself.

It turned out to be the greatest and most significant performance she ever gave in her life. It was filmed and recorded for posterity. An entire book could be devoted to this one performance alone. Anyone who was anyone in Paris was there, including the sea of reporters and photographers who had come to witness the fulfilment of her own prophecy that she would die on the stage.

As the big red curtain swung back, the audience saw nothing but total darkness. The orchestra struck up *L'hymne à l'amour*, and a miracle occurred as Edith emerged slowly from the back of the stage and approached the spotlight. The crowd rose in one body and applauded her madly for almost half an hour. Then, with a single movement of her tiny deformed hands – hands which Cocteau had once described as lizardous – she silenced them and announced her first song, said to be based on the Cerdan theme, *Les mots d'amour*, on the soundtrack of the boxing film, *Un cœur gros comme ça* in 1968.

> C'est fou c'qu'il me disait comme jolis mots d'amour,
> Et comme il les disait!
> Mais il ne s'est pas tué,
> Car malgré son amour, c'est lui qui m'a quitte!
>
> (It's mad, the way he said such lovely words of love,
> And how he said them!
> But he didn't kill himself,
> Because in spite of his love, it was he who left me!)

The song reminds the listener of a major Piaf philosophy: dying for love. It occurred in her next song, *Les flons-flons du bal*, too, for amidst the boisterous sounds of the street-dancing, there is an interlude in which she confides,

> J'ai bien failli mourir,
> Le jour où t'es parti . . .
>
> (I almost died,
> The day you went away . . .)

The third recorded song, the self-composed *T'es l'homme qu'il me faut*, is in a way reminiscent of Edith's summer affair in Cannes with Douglas Davis, and is unusually optimistic:

> Quand j'sors avec toi,
> J'm'accroche à ton bras,
> Les femmes, elles te voient,
> Toi, tu n'les vois pas,
> T'es l'homme qu'il me faut!
>
> (When I go out with you,
> I hang onto your arm.
> Women see you,
> But you don't see them,
> You must be the man for me!)

There is an interesting anecdote connected with *Mon Dieu*, by Vaucaire and Dumont, which typifies Edith's determination to get exactly what she wanted. Dumont had brought her the song several weeks before the Olympia. Then it had been unimpressively entitled *Toulon-Le Havre-Anvers*. Delighted with the music, Edith had expressed such dissatisfaction with the lyrics that she had telephoned Michel Vaucaire at four in the morning, *demanding* a new lyric in time for her rehearsal at five that very afternoon! Naturally, the lyricist had obliged, and what began as a monumental headache became a resounding success. *Mon Dieu*, with its simple, heart-felt message and the backing of a choir and single solo voice – usually a weakening factor with Piaf songs – was one of her most highly acclaimed songs.

> Mon Dieu!
> Même si j'ai tort,
> Laissez-le moi encore!
>
> (Please God!
> Even if I'm wrong,
> Let me have him again!)

Edith had despaired over her next song, *Mon vieux Lucien*. Said to be based on an episode in the life of Lucien Vaimber, her chiropractor, it tells the story of a man about to kill himself, only to be saved from suicide by an old friend. Dumont's music presented few problems; it was slightly reminiscent of her earlier *La goualante du pauvre Jean*. Michel Vaucaire's lyrics were, however, tricky, and like many of her songs of the thirties were written in a kind of tongue-twisting *argot*. After only a few bars Edith forgot the words, stopped the orchestra, and laughed over her mistake with the audience, telling them that she made the same mistake at rehearsals. She began again to a rapturous applause. Parisian audiences tend to be super-critical, and no other singer would have got away with it. Piaf, however, could do no wrong, and would indeed have been able to sing the contents of a telephone directory, as someone once suggested. Later, she refused to omit the song from the recording of the recital because she claimed that she, like anyone else, was capable of making mistakes.

La ville inconnue must have reminded many people of Edith's 'suicide tour'. Each town seems like the last, with endless streets and deserted boulevards, where one wanders around like a lost dog, wanting only to sleep away each day.

> Il y a des passants,
> Qui ont l'air de vous fuir,
> Et qui n'ont pas le temps,
> De vous faire un sourire . . .
>
> (There are passers-by,
> Who seem to avoid you,
> And who haven't the time,
> To give you a smile . . .)

The supreme triumph of Olympia '61 was, of course, *Non je ne regrette rien*. After surviving countless broken love affairs, four car crashes, numerous major operations, cures for alcoholism and drug addiction, and now with the threat of death hanging over her like a low, black cloud, she stood

defiantly and proclaimed, 'I regret nothing. It's all behind
me. I'm going back to zero!'

> Avec mes souvenirs,
> J'ai allumé le feu,
> Mes chagrins, mes plaisirs,
> Je n'ai plus besoin d'eux!
>
> (I've lit a fire with my memories,
> My griefs, my pleasures,
> I no longer need them!)

La belle histoire d'amour, a pastiche of unrequited love and
hope, and a long song, was the last to be written by Edith in
memory of Marcel Cerdan.

> Je cherche à t'oublier,
> Mais c'est plus fort que moi,
> Je me fais déchirer,
> Je n'appartiens qu'à toi . . .
>
> (I seek to forget you,
> But this thing's stronger than me,
> I tear myself apart,
> I belong to no one but you . . .)

The album of the Olympia performance contains just
nine songs, and the applause between these had to be edited
because it was often longer than the songs themselves. Edith
sang a dozen or so of her older hits, including *Milord* and *La
foule*. But the phrase 'once more with feeling' could have
been invented just for her last song, *Les blouses blanches*.
It was by far the most disturbing song she ever sang – it had
far-reaching effects on at least one member of a subsequent
audience, who collapsed in the auditorium and had to be
carried out on a stretcher. Like that other masterpiece of
melodrama, *Légende*, it was only performed on the Olympia
stage, never in the studio. It was also Marguerite Monnot's
last song for Piaf, with lyrics by Michel Rivgauche.

The 'white-coats' are the warders in the lunatic asylum . . .

She's been locked up with the lunatics for eight years. It's because of the white-coats that she's there. They keep telling her she isn't insane, but she remembers a white dress she once had — a pretty dress with flowers. Then, a hand held hers, a beautiful hand with fingers which sang. But she isn't insane! She will go on loving – for ever!

Edith more than sang the song. She *acted* it, just as the great tragedienne Damia acted *La chanson du fou* whilst tearing at her hair, thirty years before. At the end of the song Edith almost became mad herself, screaming with maniacal laughter, 'I'm not insane! I'm not insane!' This song alone won her twenty-two curtain calls, and at the end of the performance she was showered with flowers.

The actual recording of the performance has sold tens of millions of copies worldwide, and continues to be re-released. One of Douglas Davis' paintings appeared on the original sleeve. Two of the songs – *Non je ne regrette rien* and *Mon Dieu* – were record successes for Piaf in English, and she even taped a German version of the former. Several years later Charles Dumont recorded them himself, and *Souviens-Toi*, a revamped version of *Les flons-flons du bal*, with Edith's voice blending in with his own, was his own personal tribute, released to coincide with the twentieth anniversary of her death. *La ville inconnue* and *Les blouses blanches* were translated for a London revue, *Edith Piaf je vous aime*. They became 'Strange Town' and 'The White-Shirts'.

As for the Olympia, it had been saved. Edith's contract was extended, and if she was dying then at least she came alive each time she stepped up to footlights to breathe in the undying love of her audiences. Indeed, at this stage in her career it seemed that she might go on for ever. Between January and April 1961 she recorded sixteen songs, again mostly by Dumont, Vaucaire, Rivgauche and Louis Poterat. Notable exceptions were *Toujours aimer*, written some time before by Marguerite Monnot and Nita Raya, and one of the few not written especially for her; *Exodus*, the Hebrew *chesed* from the film of the same name – a difficult song which unusually for her took several takes and a lot of patience – had French words by Eddy Marnay. Two songs were not released commercially until after her death because of their poor sound quality, though as usual Piaf's performance was exceptional. These were *Quand tu dors*, a poem by Jacques Prévert, and Jacques Larue's poignant *Les bleuets d'azur*.

The soundtrack for the ballet *La Voix* was also recorded at about this time, with music by Claude Leveille and lyrics by Edith and Michel Rivgauche. This time the orchestra leader was Christian Chevalier, who later worked with Nana Mouskouri and Mouloudji. It was not given its television première until 1965. It was created by the dancer-choreographer Pierre Lacotte, and the set designer was Pierre Clayette. In all, twelve songs were written for Edith to perform without being seen on the stage, and she apparently took the idea very seriously, working off and on with the team for several months. Three of the songs (*Kiosque à journaux*, *Le métro de Paris*, *Non la vie n'est pas triste*) were taped during a rehearsal. As a tribute to Edith, in 1965 the remaining songs were performed by a choir. Robert Chauvigny was still directing Edith off and on. Later, for obvious health reasons, he had to be replaced by Jean Leccia, and, in 1963, by Noël Commaret.

On 13 April 1961 Edith closed at the Olympia and went on tour. It was too much for her. On 25 May she collapsed and was admitted to the American Hospital at Neuilly, where an operation was performed for intestinal adhesions. There followed yet another convalescence with Louis Barrier at his house in Richebourg. Then on 9 June she suffered a relapse and was readmitted to the hospital with an internal blockage.

As if this was not enough, her great friend of twenty-five years, Marguerite Monnot, died suddenly of suspected peritonitis.

Edith was heart-broken. Marguerite Monnot was probably the only person in the world who really knew Piaf the *woman*. Yet they had been as different as chalk and cheese. Edith, though one of the highest-paid women in France, was no different, class-wise, at the height of her fame than she had been in the early thirties. She was still the little-girl-lost from Belleville, roughly spoken, hard as nails, incredibly down to earth with absolutely no airs and graces. Marguerite on the other hand was sophisticated, refined, and well educated. On more than one occasion Edith had made her blush in public – though once they had sung together, at a private function, the filthiest version imaginable of *Mon légionnaire* – what a pity that the alleged recording of this has been lost!

Marguerite Monnot was a very private person – almost reclusive – which must have been daunting for her if one considers the demands which Edith made on everyone, expecting composers and lyricists to be at her beck and call twenty-four hours a day.

Absent-minded often to the point of absurdity, Marguerite had usually travelled between her home and Edith's apartment on her *mobylette*, often losing it en route. In an exclusive interview for BBC radio's *Portrait of Piaf*, the film director Marcel Blistène recounted an interesting anecdote: one day Marguerite had been listening to a piece of music, or a song. Infatuated by its beauty and intensity, she had demanded the name of the composer. Blistène had quietly told her – Marguerite Monnot.

Edith mourned her friend privately, perhaps feeling more than a little guilty that she had allowed only one Monnot song to be included in her Olympia recitals. Now she told her friends, 'Never speak to me of Marguerite again.'

In a radio interview she said,

I refuse to believe in her death. Marguerite is not dead. She is still amongst us. She is beside me. She is listening to me. I will find her again, one day.

At the boulevard Lannes, the parties were still as wild as ever, even though the *patronne* was often tired. Besides the ever-present household staff, Claude Figus, and one or two hangers-on, there were Edith's old friends who dropped in. Charles Aznavour, Henri Contet, Michel Emer, Suzanne Flon, Marlene, and occasionally Raymond Asso, still bearing a grudge after twenty years.

Edith was quietly launching Claude Figus' recording career and working with him on his new songs, *Quand l'amour est fini* and *La robe bleue*, though these would never amount to much. Figus was a better secretary than he was a singer.

Figus was, at this stage in her life, something of a consolation. Though he often boasted of once being her lover, he is said to have been bisexual. He sometimes mixed with a curious crowd, and frequently took boys back to the apartment.

One of these was a handsome young Greek hairdresser. His name was Theophanis Lamboukas.

11

The Right to Love

During her convalescence at Richebourg, Edith almost
became a recluse. Only a handful of people were allowed
near her, besides the household staff from the boulevard
Lannes. One of these was her friend, Jean Noli, a reporter
who was working for *France-Dimanche*. Initially he and his
photographer, Hughes Vassal, had visited her apartment in
search of sensationalism – never too far away where Piaf
was concerned. They had become good friends, and for the
last years of her life these two men spent a lot of time with
her. Noli collected anecdotes; Vassal took some very moving
pictures. Several years after Edith's death some of these were
included in Noli's book, *Edith Piaf: trois ans pour mourir*,
perhaps the most honest account of her final years to date.

Edith opened her heart to Jean Noli – something she
rarely did – and these recollections, listed under tabloid-type
headings as though she were mocking the media for getting
things wrong before, were assembled to form her second
autobiography, *Ma vie*. The book did not cause much of a stir
when first published; much of the information was collated
between relapses in her health, and many people wondered
how much of her story was real, and how much the result of
her vivid imagination. On careful inspection, now that more
facts are known about her life, there is no reason to believe it
wasn't true. Edith knew that she was living on borrowed time;
she wanted to go to her maker with a clear conscience.

Another man almost eternally present during these last
years was her chiropractor, Lucien Vaimber, without whose
treatment she most certainly would have died earlier than she
did. At first Vaimber had been reluctant to treat her, knowing
of her disinclination to follow medical advice. Twelve years

135

later, when Guillaume Hanoteau wrote the chiropractor's biography, he called it *Les doigts du miracle*, and quite rightly so.

Charles Dumont was still Edith's favourite composer. Thinking solely of her health – and because of personal issues there could have been no romantic attachment even if Edith had wanted this, and she certainly did not – he asked her to accompany him on a skiing holiday in January 1962. She was sorely lacking a man in her life, and for more than two years had lived in a somnambulant trance, drifting between theatres and hospitals, often on the brink of death. Not only did she refuse to go on holiday with him, she forbade him to leave Paris, vowing that if he left her now he would be banished from the boulevard Lannes for good.

Dumont left, and Edith was as good as her word, for a few months at least. There was no shortage of good composers. She engaged the talents of Michelle Vendôme and Florence Véran, and was introduced to Francis Lai and Noël Commaret. Michel Emer, that faithful old soldier, was never far away.

In February 1962 she was taken to the Ambroise Paré Clinic at Neuilly, suffering from double bronchial pneumonia. She had probably forgotten Claude Figus' handsome young Greek friend, Theophanis Lamboukas: after their first meeting she had dismissed him as morose and brooding. He had perched on the edge of the sofa, twiddling his thumbs and seemingly lost for words – not surprising, really, if one considers Edith's all-powerful aura, and her insistence that all visitors to her court should be cheerful and spirited, which she certainly always was, ill or not.

Now Theophanis took to visiting her at the clinic. Instead of buying her flowers, he brought her meaningful little gifts: she was particularly touched when one day he gave her a Greek doll.

Two of Edith's former lovers had been Greeks. During visiting hours she and her young friend spoke lovingly of his homeland. Finding his name too much of a mouthful, she shortened it to Théo. He told her that he lived with his parents and two sisters above their hairdressing salon at Frette-sur-Seine, just outside Paris, and that he himself had been a hairdresser for a while. One day he asked her if he might set her hair, without knowing how sensitive she was of the fact that she hardly had any hair left. Edith agreed, and she fell in love with him!

Unlike most of his predecessors, Théo was shy, quiet, and totally unassuming. He brought books and read to her; she was still deeply into classics and adored Gide and others of that ilk. On bad days Théo spoon-fed her. Such infinite tenderness moved her. She told her friends that Théo had given her the will to live when she had thought herself beyond redemption.

One day, Théo spoke of his dream: he wanted to sing. Her recovery was nothing short of miraculous. Eleven of her lovers had become renowned internationally because of her, so why not this one? He had the looks, and more than his share of determination to succeed.

But as Theophanis Lamboukas? The theatres, she declared, would never fit his name onto their bill-boards!

As usual, Edith came up with the solution. During her romantic fling with Takis Menelas in Athens in 1946 she had picked up a few Greek words – most of them unrepeatable. Now she adapted the Greek phrase for 'I love you' which was *sarape*. Her new protégé became Théo Sarapo – 'Théo I-love-you'. And if some of her critics scoffed at the idea, she laughingly pointed out that her own name translated as 'spuggie'.

There is no doubt whatsoever – Théo Sarapo gave Edith Piaf a brand new lease of life. When they met, she already had one foot in the grave. Thanks to this young man she lived another eighteen months – the happiest months of her life apart from her time with Cerdan, whom she would still mourn until the very end. Théo was Piaf's saving grace, her earthly saint. He not only taught her how to love again. He reformed her: he helped her to find her long-lost self-respect, to have pride in her appearance once more. And importantly, he softened much of her tyranny. He was not a forceful man; far from it, he was passive, and gentle as a lamb. Bearing in mind the fact that he was a close friend of Claude Figus, and in any case hardly expected any physical relationship with Edith, one might even question Théo's own sexuality. To do so would be unjust. In her biography, Simone Berteaut had the audacity to say that most of Piaf's lovers saw only the words EDITH PIAF written in lights above the bed, but even Mômone was not scathing about this one. There have also been suggestions that Théo eventually married her for her money, which is certainly untrue. Financially, she was a wreck. She was in debt now, and always would be, and in the end Théo inherited those debts. Early on in their relationship he was told that she did not have long to live. In some respects he was as naive as she was. Dreams were to be believed in: there would always be a miracle waiting around the corner.

For Edith, there was to be one final shock.

In April 1962 Douglas Davis visited Paris. Naturally, he was invited to spend a few days *chez Piaf* – she rarely bore grudges, unlike Raymond Asso, and was on good terms with most of her ex-lovers. Neither was there any rivalry or jealousy between the two young men. Douglas and Théo quickly became friends. Without being badgered into doing so, the American painted Théo's portrait. Ironically, it was his last work. On 3 June Douglas Davis' plane crashed only minutes after take-off from Orly airport. There were no survivors.

For the second time an aeroplane had robbed Edith of a loved one. Théo and her friends tried to keep the news from her, worried that another relapse might prove fatal. Edith found out, probably from Mômone, and for several days locked herself in her room, refusing to see anyone and emerging only when Théo swore on the Bible that he would never take a plane. Théo was told that some years before, whilst she had been touring the United States, she had been forewarned of an air disaster – either by her clairvoyant, or at one of the table-tapping seances – and that she had forbidden her entourage to take the flight. Incredibly, the plane *had* crashed, and many people had been killed. Théo was convinced that she had second sight, and he complied with her wishes.

Théo took her to Cannes – not a good idea, considering that she had spent a happy time there, not long before, with Douglas. They rented a suite in the Majestic Hotel. It was a perfectly unselfish act. Again she was seen in public wearing the old-fashioned swimsuit, although this time she did not have to forbid her man to leave her side . . . Théo had eyes for her alone. On 26 July he proposed to her. She was stunned. Twenty years and a great deal of experience separated them. He was young and strong and handsome enough to have any woman he wanted. She, in her own words, was an old wreck. Marriage would only make them a laughing-stock. She asked him to give her a little time to think things over, probably hoping that he would change his mind which, of course, he didn't.

For a quarter of a century cynics have asked the same question: *why?*

She was still the highest-paid female entertainer in the world, but she spent faster than she earned, and would never change. And if she had been pretty when younger, she was not so now, she said. Perhaps she had never heard of the saying, 'Beauty is in the eye of the beholder.' She measured 4 ft 7 ins, weighed 84 pounds, and was so crippled with rheumatism that she could hardly walk. Even eating was a severe trial. The doctors confirmed to Théo what he had been told by Edith's friends: at best she would live no more than a few years, and she might have to stop singing at any moment. So why did he insist on marrying her? Why not let their affair run its course like all the others, then move on?

Quite simply, he loved her. They adored each other. They were a modern-day, nonconformist Romeo and Juliet.

In August 1962 they went on a pilgrimage to Ste Thérèse's shrine at Lisieux, then on to La Frette to meet Théo's family. Here, Monsieur Lamboukas formally consented to the union, and Edith realised that she was going to have something she had never had in her life – a family. Madame Lamboukas asked Edith to call her *Maman*. This amused her, for there were only a few years between them. During this first visit, too, Théo's sisters put on a record by Richard Anthony and persuaded her to dance *le twist*!

The wedding was arranged for 9 October; and was it coincidence that it would be sixteen years to the day since she had recorded *La vie en rose* and *Mariage*? – though this latter number, in which the hapless bride goes to jail for murdering her husband, does not linger long on wedded bliss. The engagement was celebrated at Cap Ferrat with just a handful of close friends, chief of whom was now Louis Barrier.

Soon afterwards, inspired by her newly found joy, Edith began working again. Louis Barrier had arranged a series of recitals along the Côte d'Azur, to be followed by a short season at the Olympia.

As with Yves Montand, Edith insisted that Théo be given second billing. No one argued this time. Very sick, she had to be humoured if nothing else.

For several weeks she had been putting Théo through the mill, attempting to teach him the seemingly impossible – how to sing. As a *chanteur-réaliste* he was unbelievably bad. His voice was too nasal, his stance and delivery too clumsy and contrived. Louis Barrier, always fearful of Edith's delicate health and dreadful temper, had persuaded the theatre managers to take him on out of pity. Edith, however, ruled over the proceedings like a Tartar chieftain. She was so harsh towards her fiancé that it is a wonder he did not change his mind about wanting to marry her: if she was like this before they were married, what would be life like afterwards! Yet when the time came for Théo to make his first professional appearance, he astounded everyone by revealing that he actually *could* sing. Not only that, he could sing remarkably well.

The recitals were attended mostly by tourists. Théo's entire repertoire had been written by Edith – who also stage-managed the show – with music by Francis Laï, Noël Commaret, and Charles Dumont, now welcomed back into the fold, though not entirely forgiven.

Théo Sarapo's debut performances were unpretentious, sincere, and generally well received. Like Edith he quickly attracted a fairly large homosexual following, and part of his audience must have been shocked – or thrilled – when, during the fourth song he peeled off his shirt and sang bare-chested. He had a fine physique, and Edith, keeping a watchful eye on him from the wings, probably never realised the effect he was having on some people. Her husband-to-be did not have to sing a song like *Les blouses blanches* to make his fans faint. If anyone passed out during that magical fourth song, it was nothing to do with the heat, either.

One song alone proclaimed the couple's private ecstasy to the rest of the world . . . *A quoi ça sert l'amour?*

With words and music by the incomparable Michel Emer, the song was first performed on *Cinq colonnes à la une*, and it was Edith's first duet with another artiste since her duets with Eddie Constantine and Jacques Pills in the early fifties.

Théo would ask:

> A quoi ça sert l'amour?
> On raconte toujours
> Les histoires insincères.
> A quoi ça sert d'aimer?
>
> (What's the use of love?
> One always tells insincere stories.
> What's the use of loving?)

Edith's response was typically philosophical. 'You're the last! You're the first!'

And, she concluded:

> Avant toi y avait rien,
> Avec toi je suis bien,
> C'est toi qu'il me fallait!
> Toi que j'aimerai toujours,
> Ça sert à ça, l'amour!
>
> (Before you I had nothing,
> With you I'm fine,
> I must have you!
> I'll always love you,
> *That's* the use of love!)

Apparently, not everyone approved of their engagement, and some members of the media – a section of her hated *honorable société* – were far from kind. Jean Louville, writing for *Noir et Blanc* on 3 August 1962, was both heartless and debasing:

EDITH PIAF: 'MY MARRIAGE WITH
THÉO IS MY CHALLENGE TO DEATH!'

A scrap of cardboard headed HOTEL MAJESTIC, CANNES. Clumsily written words: EDITH PIAF AND THÉO SARAPO HAVE JOY IN ANNOUNCING THEIR MARRIAGE AT THE END OF OCTOBER '62. Signed by the fiancés, a distinctly exceptional, unexpected invitation. The public found it unbelievable when Edith started her 'adventure' with Théo Sarapo, but this marriage exceeds the bounds of understanding. One tries to discern why the great singer, not content with this conspicuous liaison, has to leap the ultimate hurdle and MARRY him. She could easily be his mother, and it is this enormous age difference which shocks us. He is handsome, ambitious. Like others who have become stars, he COULD take her advice and live with Edith for a while and add more to the gossip columns.

One can only repeat . . . UNBELIEVABLE!

Edith was offended, but the love and good opinion of her beloved public meant more to her than the crass ravings of an insensitive journalist. She retaliated by getting Jean Noli to place an advertisement in his newspaper, more or less asking for her public's blessing.

The article brought her literally thousands of letters and cards from well-wishers. She also gave a very frank interview to Victor Newson of the British *Daily Express*, at a time when she had once again turned down an offer to sing in Britain. She explained that in her opinion, the British understood nothing about falling in love, and that it was probably an advantage when one partner was older than the other because of his or her greater experience of life. She said that, since Théo's parents had given their seal of approval, she no longer cared what other people thought about their marriage. This journalist concluded that the love between Piaf and Sarapo was 'a love affair that France loves'.

It was true, of course, that she was old enough to be Théo's mother. Cynical tabloids of today would have branded him a 'toy boy' – and had she lived, Edith's baby daughter would have been twenty-nine, two years older than her prospective stepfather. The maternal instinct was certainly there, as Edith explains herself, in *Ma vie*:

> At forty-seven I found myself the same as I had been at sixteen, when I left my father to go and sing in the streets – alone, with fewer hopes and illusions. Théo, with his laugh, his spirit and youth gave me the impression that I had a son. A mother sleeps within even the most voluptuous of mistresses.
> I didn't deserve such happiness!

The première for Olympia '62 was firmly set for 27 September, but Edith's health was so uncertain that Louis Barrier and Bruno Coquatrix had agreed on a two-week run this time.

Two days before, Edith sang in her last gala performance in a concert from the top of the Eiffel Tower, for the première of the film, *The Longest Day*. The show was preceded by a sumptuous banquet in the Palais de Chaillot gardens, and the audience of 3000 was the most distinguished she had ever sung to – Lord Mountbatten, the Shah of Iran, Prince Rainier of Monaco, Montgomery and Churchill, Queen Sophia of Greece, Sophia Loren, Richard Burton and Elizabeth Taylor, Joseph Kessel, Audrey Hepburn, and her friend Eisenhower were but a few.

Edith sang only fourteen songs, eleven of them for the first time, including *Le diable de la Bastille, Emporte-moi, Musique à tout va*, and *Le petit brouillard* – another song with an unexpected ending, like *L'accordéoniste*, which was now dropped from her repertoire because of its exhausting range. She also sang her most portentous song, *Le droit d'aimer*, by Robert Nyel and Francis Laï. It would become her personal credo, and it was her last European hit during her lifetime.

> A la face des hommes,
> Au mépris de leurs lois,
> Jamais rien ni personne
> M'empêchera d'aimer,
> J'en ai le droit d'aimer!

(Facing men,
Scorning their laws,
Nothing . . . no one
Will prevent me from loving.
I have the right to love!)

If anyone had the right to love – through fear of losing everything and even at the risk of destroying herself, as the song indicates – Edith Piaf had.

On the opening night of Olympia '62 Edith faced dozens of press reporters and photographers, good, bad, and indifferent. That night there was no prophecy of death, only love. The audience was a tough one, even by French standards. Sheer sensationalism connected with her forthcoming marriage had attracted a curious cross-section of the public. The genuine fans were there, of course, but they were vastly outnumbered by that cynical section of Parisian society who wanted to see if she was still capable of standing on her feet. Here was her *honorable société* again, but if they were expecting the spectacle of Sarapo, *torse nu*, they were to be disappointed. Edith had given her fiancé strict instructions to keep his shirt on.

Edith excelled herself with a new repertoire of songs with a higher range than usual. *Musique à tout va*, had it been written then, might have defied her in the mid-fifties when she had been at the peak of physical fitness. Now it and her other numbers were delivered with comparative ease, though the gaps between her songs were noticeably longer: she no longer raised her hand to quieten the audience, preferring to allow the applause to run on as long as possible so that she could get her breath back.

The opening number, *Roulez tambours*, also listed as *Les tambours*, was a rare excursion, for Piaf, into the realm of protest songs:

Allez! Roulez, roulez tambours!
Pour ceux qui meurent chaque jour,
Pour ceux qui pleurent dans les faubourgs!

Pour Hiroshima!
Pearl Harbor!

(Come! Roll the drums!
For those who are dying each day,
For the ones crying in the suburbs!
For Hiroshima!
Pearl Harbor!)

When Edith bawled out for Théo to join her on the stage, there was an outburst of mocking laughter, probably because of the difference in their heights. After they had sung *A quoi ça sert l'Amour*, however, the applause spoke for itself. Publicly, their engagement had been accepted.

After the show Edith was interviewed by Pierre Desgraupes:

DESGRAUPES: After your triumph, what will happen next?

PIAF: My fight. I'm going to win because I think I'm indestructible.

DESGRAUPES: You must win . . .

PIAF: I must win. I can't ever lose!

DESGRAUPES: There's something invincible about you. A miracle. People say you're finished . . . you will never sing again. You always return. How do you explain this?

PIAF: My fight! As long as there's a breath of life within me, I'll fight!

DESGRAUPES: You've been singing for twenty-seven years, with constant success. How do you explain this?

PIAF: I've been sincere, I think, in giving all to my art. My heart . . . my life.

DESGRAUPES: You've earned – and lost – a lot of money. Don't you ever think of your old age?

PIAF: (roaring with laughter) How dreadful!

DESGRAUPES: You had an immense hit, *Non je ne regrette rien*. Do you regret nothing?

PIAF: Absolutely nothing!

DESGRAUPES: But, the tragic moments . . .

PIAF: I thank God for the joys and the pains that he has given me.

DESGRAUPES: You always sing about love. It isn't just another word to you. You've had a lot of love in your life . . .

PIAF: You can't live without love!

DESGRAUPES: You don't regret, even, the ones which deceived you?

PIAF: No one ever deceived me. I made personalities. They were as I wanted them to be.

DESGRAUPES: And . . . when it's over?

PIAF: I'll make films!

DESGRAUPES: Did any of your lovers stand out from the rest?

PIAF: Yes . . .

DESGRAUPES: May I ask which one?

PIAF: I can't mention names. There was one. He
was genuine.

DESGRAUPES: And . . . are you singing as well now as you
were fifteen years ago?

PIAF: Only the public can tell you that!

Edith's wedding on 9 October 1962 was a feast for public
and press alike. A vast crowd gathered outside the Mairie of
the 16th arrondissement. The police had to be brought in to
restore order before Edith arrived, wearing a black alpaca
dress – and her old mink coat. She resembled a fragile doll,
but was smiling radiantly. According to her nurse, Simone
Margantin – herself a close friend and confidante now that
Marguerite Monnot had gone – Edith developed cold feet a
few hours before the ceremony and had to be coaxed into
Théo's brand new white Mercedes – after her injection.

The civil ceremony was followed by a religious one at the
Greek Orthodox Church on the rue Daru. It was filmed.
Edith and Théo exchanged rings and crowns, which were
placed on their heads by Louis Barrier. They were blessed
by the same priest that had married her friend Sacha Guitry
and Lana Marconi, some years before. Outside the church,
the fanatical crowd chanted 'Vive la Mariée!' This pleased
Edith, who until then had not considered herself a typical
bride. One or two of the onlookers were interviewed by
reporters, and a variety of reasons were given for being
there. Most were genuine admirers, fighting to embrace or
even touch her during her brief walkabout. Others were there
out of curiosity, to scoff and jeer at the bridegroom, who took
their insults of 'gigolo' and '*maquereau*' on the chin, like the
mild mannered young man he was.

The couple returned to the boulevard Lannes for the
first time in several weeks. Prior to their wedding Théo had
rented a suite at the George V Hotel, having taken it upon
himself to have the apartment refurbished and made to look
like a home even if, according to Jean Noli, his tastes were
decidedly not *au fait*. He had done his best, and in any case it
was the thought that counted. The new furniture was mostly

Danish, the armchairs and divans were suitably upholstered with black velvet, and the wall coverings were of red silk. But Edith disapproved of the carpets – they were an unlucky green.

Their wedding presents to each other were equally strange. For Edith, a collection of rare first editions of Baudelaire and Balzac, and an enormous teddy-bear. The latter is now in the Piaf Museum, in the headquarters of Les Amis d'Edith Piaf in Paris. Edith bought Théo an exercise cycle and an electric train set. One of the photographs taken at the time by Hughes Vassal shows him playing with it, whilst Edith is sitting in a corner, sewing nonchalantly.

For several days, there were incessant interviews with the media. This time, Edith had little patience. It had taken her a long time to replace Cerdan – if indeed she had – and she branded the reporters as vultures. She also took some of them for a ride. One in particular amused her – the name of the interviewer, needless to say, has never been revealed.

TO THÉO: What effect will it have on you, marrying a woman twenty years your senior?

RESPONSE: Edith has the character of a child.

TO EDITH: What effect does it have on you, marrying a man twenty years younger than yourself?

RESPONSE: The effect that I was lucky, finding a man so gentle, and handsome!

TO THÉO: Will you have children?

RESPONSE: If my wife wishes. . .

TO EDITH: Do you want any children?

RESPONSE: Sure! Why not?

Soon afterwards, Edith again entered a detoxication clinic. This time, through no fault of her own, she had become dependent on the needle. It was a brief visit. When she returned to the boulevard Lannes, accompanied by Simone Margantin – from now on she would always be at her side – she seemed strong enough to take on her next venture, a tour of Holland and Belgium.

She had been booked to appear at L'Ancienne Belgique, in Brussels. It was a large, expensive cabaret noted for the noise its clientele made with their knives and forks whilst the artistes were on stage. Edith, of course, made several conditions. Charles Dumont, back in her bad books for some reason, was informed that she was going to remove *Non je ne regrette rien* from her programme as it could no longer be included on the same bill as *Le droit d'aimer*. Then, several days before she left France, Dumont found himself suddenly summoned to court. She had written a poem, *Le chant d'amour*, which she wanted setting to music. He agreed – and Edith agreed in turn to retain *Non je ne regrette rien* in her repertoire!

Le chant d'amour was the last song which Edith wrote for herself, though she wrote others for her husband. It was a great success, though she never got as far as recording it in the studio.

During the afternoon of 3 December 1962 she paid a visit to the Pathé-Marconi studios, and in one take recorded *Le rendez-vous*, by René Rouzaud and Francis Laï.

There were no more recording sessions.

The tour proved too much for her, but she stuck it out, even though she was forced to return home, twice, to be given vital blood transfusions. At L'Ancienne Belgique she sang her *Chant d'amour* – it was as though she had seen beyond her own death, for the lovers in the song both die and are reunited afterwards in heaven – and she also introduced several new songs, including *J'en ai tant vu:*

> Je croyais que j'avais tout vu,
> Tout fait, tout dit, tout entendu,
> Et je m'disais 'On n'm'aura plus!'
> C'est alors qu'il est venu!

> (I thought I'd seen everything,
> Done, said, heard everything,
> I told myself, 'Nobody wants me any more!'
> That's when he came along!)

There was little time left, and Edith still believed in miracles.

Louis Barrier booked her to appear in a series of recitals at the Bobino, and more offers poured in. She was going to tour Japan and the United States, and there was to be a performance before President Kennedy at the White House – little did the world know that they would both be dead before the year was out.

Edith opened at the Bobino on 18 February 1963, with Théo Sarapo as her *vedette-américaine*. All his songs were written by Edith, and the public observed that his act was more polished than it had been at the Olympia, even if Edith had used one of his songs, *Défense de*, to get back at her *honorable société*. His voice was still rather nasal, but his performance was dramatic and well received. Some years later one of his songs, *Les mains*, was translated into English and used in Libby Morris's London revue.

Edith's opening performance was received more hysterically than any other she ever gave. The audience, as if aware that they were hearing the Great Piaf for the last time, went mad. Six of the songs were new to her Parisian public, and years ahead of their time. *Traqué* and *Monsieur incognito* were by Robert Gall and Florence Véran. *Tiens v'là un marin!* was by Julien Bouquet, and proved that she was still fond of sailors. The catchy, sing-along *Margot cœur-gros* was by Michelle Vendôme. For some reason it was translated into English as 'Poor Little Lost Louise'. And, of course, there was *Le chant d'amour*.

One song drove the audience wild, in more ways than one. this was *C'était pas moi*, by Robert Gall and Francis Laï, which some critics declared was even more disturbing than *Les blouses blanches*, and which Edith acted out so dramatically that some of the audience thought she was having a fit. Listening to the song now certainly sends shivers down one's spine. It tells the story of a man who has been thrown into prison for a murder he did not commit, and the song really has to be heard to be believed. 'It wasn't me! It wasn't me!' Edith screams, at the top of her voice as the curtain falls.

Finally, she sang *Les gens*, a subtle slap in the face for those who still criticised her marriage.

> Comme ils baissaient les yeux, les gens,
> Comme ils nous regardaient les gens,
> Quand tous deux on s'est enlacé,
> Quand on s'est embrassé!
>
> (How people lowered their eyes,
> How people looked at us,
> When we hugged one another
> When we kissed!)

After the Bobino, Edith and Théo toured again; she was so ill, now, that it was an effort to sing more than a dozen songs. The public were ready to believe that she would last for ever: she had already said that she would never retire. And, of course, she was only forty-seven, the age when most *chanteuses-réalistes* are reaching their peak.

On 18 March 1963 Edith Piaf sang in public for the last time, at the Opera House in Lille.

She returned to the boulevard Lannes and immediately began preparing for a tour of Germany. A demonstration tape of *Non je ne regrette rien*, sung phonetically in German, had already been made, and there were to be others. Edith had never forgiven the Germans for their atrocities during the Occupation, and Michel Vaucaire and Charles Dumont had written a somewhat harrowing song about the Berlin Wall, *Le mur*. It is a fine, dramatic piece which may or may not have been taped – it has not yet come to light. A few years later it was recorded in English as well as French by Barbra Streisand.

L'homme de Berlin, by Michelle Vendôme and Francis Laï, has survived. Edith recorded it on 7 April 1963, on a bedside tape recorder at the Boulevard Lannes, accompanied by Noël Commaret on the piano and the composer on the accordion.

It is the ultimate testimony of the greatest *chanteuse-réaliste* the world has ever known.

> Sous le ciel crasseux qui pleurait d'ennui,
> Sous la petite pluie qui tombait sur lui,
> J'l'ai pris pour l'amour, c'était un passant,
> Lui, l'homme de Berlin . . .

> (Under a grimy, anxiously weeping sky,
> Under the gentle rain, which fell upon him,
> I picked him up, a passer-by,
> The man from Berlin . . .)

The German tour never took place, and Théo Sarapo kept the tape until 1968, when it was released on a French Pathé-Marconi EP with *Le diable de la Bastille*, and two of the songs from Edith's recital at the Bobino.

On 10 April Edith was rushed into the Ambroise Paré Clinic at Neuilly, where doctors diagnosed an oedema of the lung. She lapsed into a coma, and for two weeks lay on the brink of death.

She recovered sufficiently for the doctors to allow her discharge from the clinic, and Théo took her to Cap Ferrat; here he rented a villa, La Serena, initially for two months. For a little while she rallied and regained enough strength to have a violent quarrel with Claude Figus. The little secretary had revealed 'certain secrets' about her private life to the press, and one wonders what he might have revealed next, had she not sent him packing.

At La Serena Edith entertained all her old friends, and there was even talk of an Olympia '63. Charles Aznavour and Denise Gassion were regular visitors, as were Stavros and Madame Lamboukas, and Théo's sisters. Jean Noli was there most of the time, collecting information and concluding his work on *Ma vie*.

Edith was rehearsing a new song, *Je m'en remets à toi*, with music by Charles Dumont and astonishingly lovely lyrics by Jacques Brel. The song, sadly, was never recorded, and out of respect for Edith, Brel never sang it himself. He himself died two days before the fifteenth anniversary of her death, on 9 October 1978.

Throughout all this, the stalwart nurse, Simone Margantin, ruled the Piaf household like a benevolent dictator.

In June 1963 Edith sent a telegram to Raymond Asso, now well into his sixties, and himself ailing. If one is to believe the long-deposed poet, Edith was in a pretty desperate state and this was a plea from the heart, like that other one after the Leplée affair. Asso did not go to her straight away, but when he arrived at the villa in July, he was obviously shocked by what he saw:

I will not dwell on the lamentable picture that I saw. Sumptuously clean, surrounded by a band of pitiful, evil clowns, like in a Pirandello drama, I found an absolutely unrecognisable Piaf. She took me to one side. Weighing her words carefully she said, 'Raymond, it's very bad – I think I'm done for, this time. Perhaps I still have a chance – with you. Since you're free, when I return to Paris, come and live with me and rid me of all this trouble, of all these people around me.'

'All?' I asked.

'Yes,' she said. 'Except for Loulou.'

It would have delighted Asso to have had her all to himself again after so many years. It never happened, of course, and when Théo discovered what had transpired, he threatened Raymond Asso with legal action.

Meanwhile, Edith continued working, although her nurse had banned her from working through the night. Her latest protégée was Christine Lamboukas, Théo's sister. Then, because the sea air proved too much for her, her doctors advised Théo to take Edith to Gatounière, a peaceful mountain retreat near Mougins. Here, she spent the last few months of her life.

On 20 August she went into a hepatic coma and was taken to the Meridien Clinic at Cannes. Miraculously, she still clung to life. As soon as she was well enough to travel she was transferred yet again, to the village of Plascassier, near Grasse. The house, L'Enclos de la Bourre, was the most depressing place ever, though by now Edith was too sick to know or care where she was.

Meanwhile, events were taking place of which she knew little or nothing. In Paris, her great friend Jean Cocteau was very ill. Théo was away much of the time, travelling back and forth to the capital. He was working on his first film, *Judex*, directed by Georges Franju. And on 5 September the exiled Claude Figus was found dead in his hotel room. The official verdict was that he had taken an overdose of drugs, and some said he had taken his life in a fit of remorse after being ousted by Piaf. An article, printed some years later in *Paris Match*, recording the death of Théo Sarapo, suggested that Figus might even have been murdered. He certainly mixed with a rough and ready crowd.

Théo gave strict orders to the household that Edith was not to be informed of Figus' death, fearing that such a shock might kill her. Figus had been just twenty-nine. For more years than anyone cared to remember he had been Piaf's slave – her court jester. He had been the butt of her cruellest jokes, and had often taken the brunt of her sometimes unpleasant temper. Once he had been sent to prison for frying eggs for her breakfast – over the flame of the Arc de Triomphe.

At Plascassier, Simone Margantin's indomitable authority was overruled just once by Théo, and he was later to regret allowing Mômone to enter the house. She was with her daughter – 'on the cadge' as Edith put it – and at first Edith would have nothing to do with her. Théo persuaded her to see her.

According to Simone Margantin, it was but a brief encounter – a far cry from the invented account which Mômone included in her book a few years later. Edith had never forgiven her for stealing her letters to Marcel Cerdan. It was probably Mômone who told Edith of Claude Figus' death, adding, as she did in her book, that little Claude had taken his own life 'to open the gates of heaven for my sister'.

Many people firmly believe that this final, spiteful act hastened Edith's end.

The author is one of them.

On 9 October 1963 – her first wedding anniversary – Edith lapsed into a hepatic coma from which she never emerged.

Simone Margantin was sitting at her bedside when, at around midnight, her condition became critical and she suffered an internal haemorrhage. The doctor arrived at five in the morning, and confirmed the worst. Edith Piaf was dying. At noon, the secretary, Danielle Bonel, was told to summon a priest. Tragically, he did not come. A storm was brewing, and she could not get through on the telephone.

The faithful, loving nurse speaks of Edith's last moments with great tenderness. At ten minutes past one her eyes opened. They were shining. Then they closed again, and her head fell forwards.

Edith had slipped away from us.

She had once said, 'I am determined to come back to earth after my death . . .'

12

La reine de la chanson!

Sainte Thérèse did not allow Edith her last wishes. She had wanted to die in Paris, with a priest by her bedside.

She actually died on 10 October, but the newsflashes did not go out until the following day. Edith Piaf, who had loved Paris like a lover, could not die in some provincial village, severed from her second heart – the people would never have forgiven her. So Théo and Simone Margantin travelled overnight with her body in the back of an ambulance, and she was laid in state in the drawing room at the boulevard Lannes; the plaque, stating that she had died in Paris, is still above the door.

Throughout the day, French radio stations played solemn music. The world wept. Even in Moscow, where she had never sung, the people held a two-minute silence. Paris went mad with grief for this courageous little woman who, for the best part of thirty years, had been its very soul. For a decade they had believed this energy-charged soldier to be utterly invincible, immortal, even. They had shared her joys and her sorrows. They had helped her to fight her final battle; now this army of admirers steadfastly refused to believe in her death. Within hours of the first newsflash, every Piaf record in France had been bought up by bereaved fans. The boulevard Lannes was blocked by a massive crowd, chanting her name outside the railings of No. 67.

Within the apartment, Edith had been embalmed. There was a constant stream of visitors: ashen-faced friends, colleagues, and ex-lovers. Edith's entourage were alarmed. They feared a riot, as there had been at Valentino's funeral. Théo was advised to call in police reinforcements. In fact, he did exactly what his wife would have wanted him to do. He opened the doors of the apartment to the crowd – *la foule*, that contingent of unseen lovers to whom she had cried, 'I love you! You are my life!'

For two days the people filed past her coffin, draped with the French flag as a tribute to all she had done for her country during the war. In Edith's hands were an orchid and a rose.

On the morning of 11 October the television producer Louis Mollion telephoned Jean Cocteau to arrange a radio broadcast: the poet had wanted to read a personal eulogy to his great friend. By the time Mollion arrived at Milly-sur-Forêt, Cocteau too was dead. He had succumbed to a heart attack.

Cocteau had once said, 'If Piaf dies, part of me will die too.'

Edith was buried in the Père Lachaise cemetery on Monday 14 October, amidst one of the most emotional scenes Paris has ever seen. It is estimated that two million people lined the streets of the city along the funeral route, and as the cars passed by – eleven of them filled with flowers – men, women and children fell to their knees, praying and making the sign of the cross. Their devotion was extraordinary.

Within the cemetery 40,000 people jostled and clambered over the gravestones, causing no little damage. Beside the grave, a detachment from the Foreign Legion stood to attention and saluted – a year before they, like the O.A.S. after the Algerian war, had adopted *Non je ne regrette rien* as their theme song. Their enormous wreath of purple wild flowers was inscribed: *A leur Môme Piaf – La Légion*. Maurice Chevalier's wreath read: Sleep in peace, courageous little Piaf.

Edith had been a deeply religious woman, even though she had not regularly attended mass. 'The people would stare at me,' she said. Her devotion to Sainte Thérèse had been profound. Every night of her life she had prayed, like a child, on her knees. She was never seen without her crucifix, and towards the end of her life meditated each day. Her faith turned up regularly in her songs. Now, she was given the supreme insult. The Pope, in his infinite wisdom, denied her a requiem mass and Christian burial, proclaiming that she had lived a life of public sin. In an official statement the Roman Catholic Archbishop of Paris, Cardinal Feltin said:

The honours that the Church reserves for its dead cannot be rendered towards Edith Piaf because of an irregular situation. Those who have appreciated the talents of Madame Piaf are deeply moved by her sudden death. Christians aware of her faith and charity will not fail to beseech divine mercy for her soul at the sacrifice of the Mass.

A priest, Père Thouvenin, and Bishop Martin kindly offered to say prayers over her grave, to an unearthly silence. Théo was supported by Louis Barrier – and Mômone managed to worm her way to the front line of mourners. Behind them were Théo's parents and sisters, Marlene Dietrich, Charles Aznavour, Herbert and Denise Gassion, and almost every one of the 'Piaf Boys' – not in Edith's favourite blue, this time, but in black.

Then, as the flag of the Legion flapped in the warm autumnal sunshine, her coffin was lowered into the ground. In a moment's panic, the crowd surged forwards and the barriers around the 97th Division suddenly gave way. The unfortunate Bruno Coquatrix was pushed into the grave, but was unhurt.

It was over.

ooOoo

During the next few days, some five million people filed past her expensive black marble tomb. Cocteau had been buried at Milly-sur-Forêt, Marlene Dietrich being one of the chief mourners.

Edith's death must have affected Marlene deeply. She had deserted her at the most critical point in her life, and although she turned up, off and on, during the later years, she probably never forgave herself for not seeing more of Edith towards the end of her life. Since 1963 Marlene has attended no more funerals – not even that of her own husband.

Many of the old friends and retainers, alas, are gone.

Robert Chauvigny, her former musical director, died three months after Edith.

On Christmas Eve 1963 – deliberately ill-timed – the bailiffs turned up at the boulevard Lannes and drew up a list of items to be sold in order to pay off some of Edith's debts. Amongst the items seized was an abstract painting by the Russian-born artist, André Lanskoy. This was bought back by André Schoeller, the director of an art gallery in the rue de Miromesnil, who allegedly had a brief, secretive affair with Piaf during the late fifties. Schoeller had wanted to give her the painting: she had insisted on paying for it, and there was even talk of Schoeller moving in with her and her adopting his child. For the last few years of her life the painting hung over the television set in her bedroom.

Théo Sarapo was left with an immense legacy of debts. For several years he worked hard in theatres all over Europe, until most of them had been paid off. His film, *Judex*, was not a great commercial success. Another film, *Un Conte*, in which he co-starred with Michel Bouquet, fared slightly better, and he was offered a leading role in Jacques Fabbri's comedy-musical, *Les Deux Orphélines*. He should have made the big time as a singer. His voice was good, and he had learned much of his stagecraft from Edith. Without her guiding hand and influence, however, few impresarios gave him the opportunity to prove himself. In 1964 he was offered top billing at the Bobino, but he pleaded with the management to place him as *vedette-américaine* to someone else. Appallingly, there was not one artiste in France who would agree to appear with him.

On 28 August 1970 he was killed in a car crash near Limoges, and he now lies next to his wife, her father, and little Marcelle Dupont in the Père Lachaise cemetery, where, until it was stolen, the plaque bore their photographs and the inscription which has become synonymous with Les Amis d'Edith Piaf: *Toujours avec nous*. The Friends of Edith Piaf currently have their headquarters at 5 rue Crespin-du-Gast in Paris. It was founded in 1967 by a group of young admirers, but most of the committee is formed of friends, colleagues and associates of Piaf, and at the time of his death Théo Sarapo was Honorary President. The society has regular meetings, and there is an annual rally, and the *Grand Prix Edith Piaf* is a prestigious award, in France, for amateur and professional singers alike.

Edith's first husband, Jacques Pills, died of a heart attack a few weeks after Théo. His last interview had been for the BBC.

Since then, others have passed on: Simone Margantin, Paul Meurisse, René Rouzaud, Francis Blanche, Lucien Baroux, Pierre Hiegel, Michel Simon and Marcel Achard. Michel Emer, composer of more than thirty of Edith's most famous songs, died shortly after being interviewed for this book, in October 1984.

Simone Berteaut, the incorrigible and frequently obnoxious demon spirit Mômone, succumbed to a heart attack in May 1975. She had made a name for herself, and a fortune, at Edith's expense. After writing her celebrated book she wrote her autobiography, *Mômone*, and retired to Chartres with a homosexual companion. Soon afterwards he walked out on her, and she died, alone and penniless, weighed down by remorse and regrets.

There have been many tributes, and there will be many more. Marcel Blistène contributed to the BBC's *I Regret Nothing*, and has worked tirelessly ever since, promoting Edith's name worldwide. A year or so before her death Simone Berteaut sold the film rights to her famous book. The ensuing film, *Piaf*, was not a great success.– no one who had known the real Piaf expected it to be.

The British have had their triumphs, too. They, who never saw Piaf in the flesh, were the recipients of two brilliant works. *Edith Piaf, Je vous aime* was the brainchild of Libby Morris. And who will ever forget Pam Gems' tremendous success, *Piaf*, perhaps the only work to have portrayed Edith as she was, warts and all, without the slightest hint of wishing to insult her?

The last tribute to date is, of course, that superb film directed by Claude Lelouch in 1983, *Edith et Marcel*, telling the moving story of the two most potent years of her life.

There was another posthumous accolade in Paris when, in September 1981 the Mayor, Jacques Chirac, inaugurated the place Edith Piaf, at the crossing of the rue Belgrand and the rue Capitaine Ferber. It has the most delightful little bar where her songs are played non-stop, and where the walls are covered with moving portraits and the instruction, *PHOTOGRAPHIE INTERDIT*. There is also a plaque on the wall in the rue Pierre Charron, where Gerny's used to be.

ooOoo

Since 1963 there have been innumerable contenders for the Piaf crown. Performers such as Juliette Greco, Patachou and Catherine Sauvage were unique when Piaf was alive, and long may they continue the tradition. In the mid-sixties the stages of the Bobino and the Olympia were graced by three Piaf sound-alikes. Georgette Lemaire and Betty Mars interpreted songs by Dumont and Vaucaire and are still going strong. Mireille Mathieu is, of course, well known in Britain, and in 1985 she too recorded an album of Piaf classics. None of these artistes, however, will ever take her place.

The realist tradition has been continued in France by a lady of singular talent: Barbara, recognised by many as the greatest female entertainer since Piaf, and even capable of surpassing her. Barbara is essentially a very private person, and her career has never been marred by scandal. She does not emulate Piaf – she did sing one of her songs, *Un monsieur me suit dans la rue*, at L'Ecluse in 1959, but that is as far as it goes. And like Piaf, Barbara has always been reluctant to sing in Britain. This is a great pity; with the exception of Squires and Bassey, the British have no realist singers of their own.

For many people, Piaf is not dead. Her spirit and courage have been passed on to those of us who loved her. When the song *Non je ne regrette rien* was issued on a British EP shortly after her death, the anonymous writer of the sleeve notes summed her up in a single sentence. I shall always be grateful to him, or her, for the following words:

We, with Piaf, must regret nothing she did, nothing she was, only the sad, unalterable fact that she is no longer with us.

Discography

1936–45 Polydor; 1946-63 Pathé–Marconi;
1947–48 Decca (unless otherwise stated)

A guide to the recorded output of Edith Piaf with composers, lyricists, and additional details. Tape recordings {TR} and acetates {AC} are included, and 'live' recordings of songs not otherwise recorded in the studio. The dates refer to the actual recordings, and are not release dates.

1935

– October	*La java en mineur* (1) (Léo Poll, Raymond Asso, M Delmas) AC
18 December	*Les Mômes de la cloche* (1) (Decaye, Vincent Scotto)
	Les Mômes de la cloche (2)
	L'étranger (1) (Robert Malleron, Juél, Marguerite Monnot)
	L'étranger (2)
	La java de cézigue (Eblinger, Groffe)
	Mon apèro (Juél, Robert Malleron)

1936

10 January	*Les hiboux* (P Dalbret, E Joullot)
15 January	*La fille et le chien* (Borel-Clerc, Jacques Charles, Charles Pothier)
	J'suis mordue (Jean Lenoir, L Carol, R Delamare)
	Reste (Jacques Simonot, Will Léardy, P Bayle)
7 March	*Mon amant de la coloniale* (Juél, Raymond Asso)
24 March	*Fais-moi valser* (Borel-Clerc)
	La Julie jolie (Léo Daniderff, Gaston Conté
	Quand-même (Jean Wiener, Louis Potcrat, J Mario)
	Va danser (M Legay, Gaston Couté)
7 May	*Les deux ménètriers* (Jean Richepin, L Durand)
	Il n'est pas très distingué (Marc Hely, P Maye)
8 May	*Y avait du soleil* (Jean Lenoir)
23 October	*'Chand d'habits* (R Alfred, Jacques Bourgeat)
28 October	*La petite boutique* (Roméo Carlès, O Hodeige)

1937

28 January   *Le contrabandier* (Jean Villard, Raymond Asso)
Le fanion de la Légion (1) (Marguerite Monnot, Raymond Asso)
Mon légionnaire (1) (Marguerite Monnot, Raymond Asso)
Ne m'écris pas (René Cloërec, L Lagarde, J Rodor)

12 April   *Corrêqu' et regguyer* (P Maye, Marc Helly)
Dans un bouge du vieux port (A Deltour, A Liaunet)
Entre St Ouen et Clignancourt (Adelmar Sablon, A Mauprey)
Mon cœur est au coin d'une rue (Henri Coste, Albert Lasry)

24 June   *Browning* (Jean Villard, Raymond Asso)
C'est toi le plus fort (1) (René Cloërec, Raymond Asso)
Paris-Mediterranée (René Cloërec, Raymond Asso)
Un jeune homme chantait (Léo Poll, Raymond Asso)

12 November   *Ding din don* (P Dreyfus, Raymond Asso)
Le fanion de la Légion (2) Accompanied by Jacques Métèhen
Tout fout le camp (Juél, Raymond Asso)

16 November   *Le chacal* (Charles Seider, Juél, Raymond Asso)
J'entends la sirène (Marguerite Monnot, Raymond Asso)
Le mauvais matelot (1) (P Dreyfus, Raymond Asso)
Partance (Léo Poll, Raymond Asso) Duet, artiste unknown.

1938

15 March   *Le fanion de la Légion* (3) AC
Madeleine qu'avait du cœur (1) (Max d'Yresne, Raymond Asso)
Les marins ça fait des voyages (Mitty Goldin, Raymond Asso)

3 October   *C'est lui qu'mon cœur a choisi* (Max d'Yresne, Raymond Asso)
Le grand voyage du pauvre négre (René Cloërec, Raymond Asso)
Madeleine qu'avait du cœur (2) AC
Le mauvais matelot (2) AC

12 November   *Mon légionnaire* (2)

—?   *La java en mineur* (2) Full length version

1939

31 May *Les deux copains* (Borel-Clerc, Raymond Asso)
Elle dréquentait la Rue Pigalle (1) (Raymond Asso, Louis Maitrier)
Je n'en connais pas la fin (Marguerite Monnot, Raymond Asso)
Le petit monsieur triste (Marguerite Monnot, Raymond Asso)

1940

18 March *C'est la moindre des choses* (1) (Paul Misraki)
Sur une colline (Paul Misraki)

20 March *C'est la moindre des choses* (2) AC
On danse sur ma chanson (Léo Poll, Raymond Asso)
Y'en a un de trop (Edith Piaf, Marguerite Monnot)

5 April *L'accordéoniste* (1) (Michel Emer)
Elle fréquentait la rue Pigalle (2) AC
Embrasse-moi (1) (Jacques Prévert, Walberg)
Escale (1) (Marguerite Monnot, Jean Marèze)
Jimmy c'est lui (1) (Kamke, Walberg)

27 May *L'accordéoniste* (2) AC
Embrasse-moi (2) AC
Escale (2) AC
Jimmy c'est lui (2) AC

—? *C'était la premiere fois* (unknown) AC

1941

27 May *C'était un jour de fête* (1) (Edith Piaf, Marguerite Monnot)
C'est un monsieur très distingué (Edith Piaf, Louiguy)
J'ai dansé avec l'amour (Edith Piaf, Marguerite Monnot)
Où sont-ils mes petits copains? (Edith Piaf, Marguerite Monnot)
C'était un jour de fête (2) AC
Où sont-ils mes copains? (2) AC
L'homme des bars (Edith Piaf, Marguerite Monnot) This is a live recording, taken from the soundtrack of the film *Montmartre-sur-Seine*

1942

9 February *Le vagabond* (1) (Edith Piaf, Louiguy) Duet with Yvon Jean-Claude. Other artistes unknown.
? October *Les hiboux* (2) AC
13 November *Le vagabond* (2) AC

25 November *Simple comme bonjour* (Roméo Carlès, Louiguy)
Tu es partout (1) (Edith Piaf, Marguerite Monnot)
Un coin tout bleu (Edith Piaf, Marguerite Monnot) This
is a version of *Y'en a un de Trop* with new lyrics.
1 December *Le vagabond* (3) AC
11 December *Le vagabond* (4) AC
15 December *C'était une histoire d'amour* (Jean Jal, Henri Contet)
Duet with Yvon Jean-Claude.
31 December *Le disque usé* (1) (Michel Emer)
J'ai qu'a l'regarder (Edith Piaf, Alex Siniavine)

1943

2 January *Je ne veux plus laver la vaiselle* (unknown) AC
8 January *Le brun et le blond* (Marguerite Monnot, Henri Contet)
C'était si bon (unknown) AC
La valse de Paris (unknown) AC
12 January *Ses mains* (unknown) AC
18 January *Le disque usé* (2) AC
Tu es partout (2) AC
14 April *Chanson d'amour* (unknown) AC
Monsieur Saint-Pierre (Johnny Hess, Henri Contet)
24 April *Histoires de cœur* (Marguerite Monnot, Henri Contet)
—? *C'est l'histoire de Jésus* (unknown)
—? *Mon amour vient de finir* (Edith Piaf, Marguerite
Monnot)
The last two songs were performed at the ABC
music-hall. The latter was written especially for Damia,
and both songs were probably recorded on acetate though
they have not, as yet, come to light.

1944

20 January *Un monsieur me suit dans la rue* (Jacques Besse,
Lechanois)
21 January *Coup de grisou* (Louiguy, Henri Contet)
27 January *Le chasseur de l'hotel* (Henri Bourtayre, Henri Contet)
C'est toujours la même histoire (Daniel White, Henri
Contet)
4 July *Les deux rengaines* (Henri Bourtayre, Henri Contet)
Y a pas de printemps (Marguerite Monnot, Henri Contet)

1945

13 May *Les gars qui marchaient* (Marguerite Monnot, Henri
Contet)
14 May *Celui qui ne savait pas pleurer* (Claude Normand, Henri
Contet)
Il riait (Barthole, Henri Contet)

Regarde-moi toujours comme ça (Marguerite Monnot, Henri Contet)
26 June *De l'autre côté de la rue* (Michel Emer)
? June *Escale* (3) Orchestra directed by Guy Luypaerts

1946

23 April *Adieu mon cœur* (Henri Contet, Marguerite Monnot)
C'est merveilleux (Henri Contet, Marguerite Monnot)
Le chant du pirate (Henri Contet, Marguerite Monnot)
25 June *Céline* (Traditional, arr Marc Herrand, Louis Liebard)
Dans les prisons de Nantes (Traditional)*
La complainte du roi renaud (Traditional)*
Le roi a fait battre tambour (Traditional)*
Les trois cloches (Jean Villard, arr Marc Herrand)*
9 October *Je m'en fous pas mal* (Michel Emer)
Mariage (Marguerite Monnot, Henri Contet)*
Un refrain courait dans la rue (Robert Chauvigny, Edith Piaf)
La vie en rose (Edith Piaf, Louiguy)
7 December *C'est toi le plus fort* (2) New arrangement, performed live on French radio.
La fille en bleue (Traditional, arr Marc Herrand) Live recording, venue not known.*

*Sung with Les Compagnons de la Chanson.

1947

? February *Les cloches sonnent* (Marguerite Monnot, Edith Piaf)
Le geste (Michel Emer)
Monsieur Ernest a réussi (Michel Emer)
Si tu partais (Michel Emer)
7 February *Sophie* (Norbert Glanzberg, Edith Piaf)
Une chanson à trois temps (Anna Marly)
6 October *Douce nuit* (F Gruber, Jean Brousolle) AC, possibly sung with Les Compagnons de la Chanson
Qu'as tu fait John? (Michel Emer)*
7 October *Un homme comme les autres* (Pierre Roche, Edith Piaf)*
C'est pour ça (Marguerite Monnot, Henri Contet) Sung with Les Compagnons de la Chanson*

*Pathé-Marconi

1948

11 June *Les amants de Paris* (Léo Ferre, Eddy Marnay)*
Il pleut (Pierre Roche, Charles Aznavour)*
Monsieur Lenoble (Michel Emer)*
12 July *Monsieur X* (Roger Gaze, Michel Emer)
Les vieux bateaux (Jacqueline Batell, Jacques Bourgeat)

21 July   *Il a chanté* (Cécile Didier, Marguerite Monnot) Duet with unknown artiste.*

6 August   *Amour du mois de mai* (Walberg, Jacques Larue)
Cousu de fil blanc (Michel Emer)*

*Pathé-Marconi

1949

3 February   *Dany* (Edith Piaf, Marguerite Monnot)
Paris (A Bernheim)
Le prisonnier de la tour (Gerard Calvi, Francis Blanche)

9 February   *Pour moi toute seule* (Philippe Gerard, Flavien Monod, Guy Lafarge)

1 March   *Bal dans ma rue* (Michel Emer)

? April   You're too dangerous Chéri (Louiguy, Edith Piaf) First English translation of *La vie en rose*, sung on stage at the Copacabana, Paris, accompanied by Daniel White.

21 July   *L'orgue de amoureux* (André Varel, Francis Carco, Charly Bailly)
Pleure pas (Aime Barelli, Henri Contet)

1950

2 May   *Hymne à l'amour* (Edith Piaf, Marguerite Monnot)

11 May   *La petite marie* (Edith Piaf, Marguerite Monnot)

19 June   *Le ciel est fermé* (Marguerite Monnot, Henri Contet)
Tous les amoureux chantent (J Jeepy, Marguerite Monnot)

20 June   *La fête continue* (Michel Emer)
Il fait bon de t'aimer (Norbert Glanzberg, Jacques Plante)
Le chevalier de Paris (Angele Vannier, Philippe Gerard)
Grand Prix du Disque 1952.

7 July   *C'est de la faute à tes yeux* (Edith Piaf, Robert Chauvigny)
C'est un gars (Pierre Roche, Charles Aznavour)

8 July   Hymn to Love (1) (Marguerite Monnot, Edith Piaf, Eddie Constantine)
The Three Bells (Jean Villard, Bert Reisfeld)
La vie en rose (1) (Louiguy, Edith Piaf, Mac David)

10 July   *Il y avait* (Charles Aznavour, Pierre Roche)
Simply a Waltz (Norman Wallace) An original song, never sung in French, written for Piaf to sing before General Eisenhower.

11 July   Don't Cry (1) (*C'est de la faute à tes yeux*) (Edith Piaf, Eddie Constantine)
'Cause I Love You (1) (*Du matin jusqu'au soir*) (Edith Piaf, Eddie Constantine)

—? *Je n'attends plus rien* (L Cazaux, Guillermin, Meleville)
Le dénicheur (Léo Daniderff, Gibert, Agel)
These two songs were taped during a rehearsal and extracts were included on a private LP in 1973.
Les feuilles mortes (Jacques Prévert, Joseph Kosma) AC

1951

6 April   *Demain il fera jour* (Marguerite Monnot, Marcel Achard)
11 April   *Du matin jusqu'au soir* (Edith Piaf)
L'homme que j'aimerais (Marguerite Monnot, Marcel Achard)
13 April   *Avant l'Heure* (Marguerite Monnot, Marcel Achard)
Rien de rien (Charles Aznavour, Pierre Roche)
Si si si (Marguerite Monnot, Marcel Achard) Duet with Eddie Constantine
5 May   *C'est toi* (1) (Marguerite Monnot, Edith Piaf) Duet with Eddie Constantine
C'est toi (2) As above, sung in English and French.
Chanson bleue (Marguerite Monnot, Edith Piaf)
La valse de l'amour (Marguerite Monnot, Edith Piaf)
4 July   *Chante-moi* (Edith Piaf) Duet with M. Jiteau.
Une enfant (Robert Chauvigny, Charles Aznavour)
15 October   *Je hais les dimanches* (Florence Véran, Charles Aznavour)
Padam, padam (Norbert Glanzberg, Henri Contet)
Plus bleu que tes yeux (Charles Aznavour)
8 November   *La chanson de Catherine* (Youri, Joumiaux, Pierre Damine) Prix Edith Piaf, Concours de Deauville, 1951.
Jezebel (Wayne Shanklin, Charles Aznavour)
La rue aux chansons (Michel Emer)
23 November   *A l'enseigne de la fille sans cœur* (Gilles)
Le noël de la rue (Marc Heyral, Henri Contet)
25 November   *Télégramme* (Michel Emer)

1952

28 June   *Au bal de la chance* (Norbert Glanzberg, Jacques Larue)
Je t'ai dans la peau (Gilbert Bécaud, Jacques Pills)
Mon ami m'a donné (Claude Valery, Raymond Asso)
3 September   *Elle a dit* (Gilbert Bécaud, Edith Piaf)
Ça gueule ça madame (Gilbert Bécaud, Edith Piaf) Duet with Jacques Pills.
Monsieur et Madame (Michel Emer)
Notre-Dame de Paris (Marc Heyral, Eddy Marnay)

1953

18 May *Les amants de Venise* (1) (Marguerite Monnot, Jacques Plantes)
Les amants de Venise (2)
Bravo pour le clown (Louiguy, Henri Contet)
Les croix (Gilbert Bécaud, Louis Amade)
Jean et Martine (Michel Emer)
Pour qu'elle soit jolie ma chanson (Louiguy, Edith Piaf) Duet with Jacques Pills.

11 December *Et moi* (Michel Emer)
N'y vas pas Manuel (Michel Emer)
Sœur Anne (Michel Emer)

14 December *L'effet qu'tu me fais* (Marc Heyral, Edith Piaf)

24 December *Heureuse* (Marguerite Monnot, René Rouzaud)
Johnny tu n'es pas un ange (Johnny is the Boy for Me) (Traditional Rumanian folk song, arranged by Les Paul, Paddy Roberts and Marcel Stellman, with French words by Francis Lemarque)

1954

16 February *La Goualante du pauvre Jean* (Marguerite Monnot, René Rouzaud)

10 April *Le 'Ça Ira'* (Ladrè, Bécourt, arranged by J Francaix)

20 October *Avec ce soleil* (1) (Philippe Gerard, Jacques Larue)
Avec ce soleil (2) With choral accompaniment.
Sous le ciel de Paris (1) (Hubert Giraud, Jean Drejac)
Sous le ciel de Paris (2) With choral accompaniment.

27 October *Enfin le printemps* (Marguerite Monnot, René Rouzaud)
Mea culpa (Michel Rivgauche, Hubert Giraud)

23 November *L'homme au piano* (Henning & Terningsohn, Jean-Claude Darnal)

24 November *Retour* (G Manet, Jean-Marie, Jo Heyne)

13 December *Sérénade du pavé* (Jean Varney)

1955

27 January *L'accordéoniste* (3) Live version, recorded at the Paris Olympia.
Légende (Edith Piaf, Gilbert Bécaud) Live version, Paris Olympia.
Y a pas de printemps (2) Longer version with extra verse/chorus, recorded at the Paris Olympia.

28 February *C'est à Hambourg* (Marguerite Monnot, Michelle Senlis, Claude Délècluse)
Le chemin des forains (Henri Sauget, Jean Dréjac)
Miséricorde (Philippe Gerard, Jacques Larue)
Un grand amour qui s'achève (Edith Piaf, Marguerite Monnot)

1956

8 February   *Les amants d'un jour* (Marguerite Monnot, Michelle Senlis, Claude Délècluse)
Soudain une vallée (Biff Jones, Charles Meyer, Jean Dréjac) Original title, Suddenly There's a Valley.

28 February   *L'homme à la moto* (Jerry Lieber, Mike Stoller, Jean Dréjac) Original title Black Denim Trousers and Motor-Cycle Boots.

8 March   *Avant nous* (Marguerite Monnot, René Rouzaud)

20 June   *Toi qui sais* (Michel Emer)
Une dame (Michel Emer)

4 July   *Et pourtant* (Michel Emer, Pierre Brasseur)
Marie la Française (1) (Philippe Gerard, Jacques Larue)
Marie la Française (2)

11 July   Heaven Have Mercy (*Miséricorde*) (Philippe Gerard, Rick French)
One Little Man (*Le petit homme*) (Philippe Gerard, Rick French)
My Lost Melody (*Je n'en connais pas la fin*) (Marguerite Monnot, Raymond Asso, Harold Rome)

—?   Autumn Leaves (1) (*Les feuilles mortes*) (Jacques Prévert, Joseph Kosma, Johnny Mercer)*
Chante-moi (Edith Piaf, Mac David)*
I Shouldn't Care (*Je m'en fous pas mal*) (Michel Emer, Rick French)*
La vie en rose (2)* Don't Cry (2)*
'Cause I Love You (2)* Hymn to Love (2)*

*Recorded in English or English/French, possibly during a visit to the United States.

1957

13 January   *C'est pour ça* (2)
*Je t'ai dans la peau**
Lovers for a Day (*Les amants d'un jour*) (Marguerite Monnot, Rick French)*
*Les grognards** Autumn Leaves (2) Rearranged version, The Highway (*Un jeune homme chantait*) (Léo Poll, Raymond Asso,?)*
*Heureuse** If You Love Me Really Love Me (*Hymne à l'amour*) (Marguerite Monnot, Edith Piaf, Geoffrey Parsons)
La vie en rose (3) Rearranged English/French version.

All the above were recorded live during a performance at Carnegie Hall. Songs marked were sung in English or English/French. Unless stated, the lyricists are not known.

25 November   *La foule* (Angel Cabral, Michel Rivgauche)
Les grognards (Hubert Giraud, Pierre Delanoë) Studio version.
Opinion publique (Marguerite Monnot, Henri Contet)
Les prisons du roi (Irving Gordon, Michel Rivgauche) Original title, Allentown Jail.
Salle d'attente (Marguerite Monnot, Michel Rivgauche)
7 November   *Comme moi* (Michelle Senlis, Claude Délècluse, Marguerite Monnot)

1958

21 March   *Mon manége à moi* (Norbert Glanzberg, Jean Constantin)
27 March   *Les amants de demain* (Marguerite Monnot, Henri Contet)
Fais comme si (Marguerite Monnot, Michel Rivgauche)
3 July   *Le ballet des cœurs* (Norbert Glanzberg, Michel Rivgauche)
Un étranger (1) (Georges Moustaki, Norbert Glanzberg) AC, superseded by the later version.
2 September   *Les neiges de Finlande* (Marguerite Monnot, Henri Contet)
Tant qu'il y aura des jours (Marguerite Monnot, Michel Rivgauche)
3 September   *C'est un homme terrible* (Jean-Pierre Moulin)
Le gitan et la fille (Georges Moustaki)
Eden Blues (Georges Moustaki)
Les orgues de barbarie (Georges Moustaki)
Un étranger (2) (Georges Moustaki, G Evan, Robert Chauvigny)
4 September   *Je me souviens d'une chanson* (Jean-Pierre Moulin, Félix Marten)
Je sais comment (Julien Bouquet, Robert Chauvigny)
Tatave (Albert Simonin, Henri Crolla)

1959

–? January   *Faut pas qu'il se figure* (1) (Lyrics by Michel Rivgauche) According to the Pathé-Marconi lists this song had original music by Georges Moustaki, although the limited edition LP of 1973 (*Inedits et Documents*) states that the tape recording was made in 1961, with music by Charles Dumont.
5 August   *Milord* (Marguerite Monnot, Georges Moustaki)
T'es beau tu sais (Georges Moustaki, Henri Contet)

1960

13 May *C'est l'amour* (Marguerite Monnot, Edith Piaf)
Ouragan (Claude Leveille, Michel Rivgauche)

20 May *Les amants merveilleux* (Robert Gall, Florence Véran)
Cri du cœur (Henri Crolla, Jacques Prévert)
Je suis à toi (Julien Bouquet)
Le vieux piano (Claude Leveille, Henri Contet)

27 May *Boulevard du crime* (Claude Leveille, Michel Rivgauche)
Le long des quais
Rue de Siam
The above two songs are included in the Pathé-Marconi list, but have never been released on record. The lyricists and composers are not mentioned.

10 November *Non je ne regrette rien* (Michel Vaucaire, Charles Dumont)
La vie, l'amour (Michel Rivgauche, Robert Chauvigny)

24 November *Jérusalem* (Jo Moutet, Robert Chabrier)
Les mots d'amour (Michel Rivgauche, Charles Dumont)

12 December *Des histoires* (Michel Vaucaire, Charles Dumont)
Mon dieu (Michel Vaucaire, Charles Dumont)

15 December *Je m'imagine* (Marguerite Monnot, Nita Raya)
La ville inconnue (Michel Vaucaire, Charles Dumont)

22 December *Les flons-flons du Bal* (Michel Vaucaire, Charles Dumont)
T'es l'homme qu'il me faut (Edith Piaf, Charles Dumont)
La belle histoire d'amour (Edith Piaf, Charles Dumont)

29 December *Les blouses blanches* (Marguerite Monnot, Michel Rivgauche) Recorded live at the Paris Olympia.

—? *Kiosque à journaux* (Pierre Lacotte, Michel Rivgauche, Claude Leveille)
Le métro de Paris (Pierre Lacotte, Michel Rivgauche, Claude Leveille)
Non la vie n'est pas triste (Edith Piaf, Claude Leveillé)
The above three songs were recorded on tape, and released posthumously. They are extracts from the ballet, *La voix*.

1961

25 January *Dans leur baiser* (Michel Vaucaire, Charles Dumont)
Mon vieux Lucien (Michel Rivgauche, Charles Dumont)
Toujours aimer (Nita Raya, Charles Dumont)

3 February *Exodus* (Ernest Gold, Eddy Marnay) From the film of the same name.
Marie Trottoir (Michel Vaucaire, Charles Dumont)

2 March   *Le billard electrique* (Louis Poterat, Charles Dumont)
Faut pas qu'il se figure (2) (Michel Rivgauche, Charles Dumont)

13 March   *Mon Dieu* (Dallas, Charles Dumont) Sung in English
No Regrets (*Non je ne regrette rien*) (Hal David, Charles Dumont)

23 March   *Le bruit des villes* (Louis Poterat, Charles Dumont)
C'est peut-être ça (Michel Vaucaire, Charles Dumont)

4 April   Carmen's Story (Michel Rivgauche, Charles Dumont)
Qu'il etait triste cet Anglais (Louis Poterat, Charles Dumont) Sung partly in English.

—? May   *Non je ne regrette rien* (Charles Dumont, lyricist not known) Tape recording, sung in German.
Quand tu dors (Jacques Prévert, C Verger) TR with background noise.
Les bleuets d'azur (Jacques Larue, Guy Magenta) TR

17 May   *Les amants* (Edith Piaf, Charles Dumont) Duet with Charles Dumont.

1962

26 January   *Fallait-il* (Michel Vaucaire, Charles Dumont)
Toi tu l'entends pas (Pierre Delanoë, Charles Dumont)

15 February   *Polichinelle* (Jacques Plante, Charles Dumont)
Une valse (Jacques Plante, Charles Dumont)

22 February   *Ça fait drôle* (Jacques Plante, Charles Dumont)
On cherche un Auguste (Robert Gall, Charles Dumont)

19 April   *Inconnu excepté de Dieu* (Louis Amade, Charles Dumont) Duet with Charles Dumont.

20 April   *Les amants de Téruel* (Jacques Plante, Mikis Theodorakis)
Quatorze Juillet (Jacques Plante, Mikis Theodorakis) The above two songs are taken from the soundtrack of the film, *Amants de Téruel*.

4 May   *Le petit brouillard* (Jacques Plante, Francis Laï)

3 September   *A quoi ça sert l'amour* (Michel Emer) Duet with Théo Sarapo.
Emporte-moi (Jacques Plante, Francis Laï)
Musique à tout va (René Rouzaud, Francis Laï)

20 September   *Le diable de la Bastille* (Pierre Delanoë, Charles Dumont)
Le droit d'aimer (1) (Robert Nyèl, Francis Laï) Orchestra directed by Jean Léccia.

21 September   *Roulez tambours* (Edith Piaf, Francis Laï) Listed on some recordings simply as *Les tambours*.

13 November   *Le droit d'aimer* (2) Orchestra directed by Robert Chauvigny.

3 December   *Le rendez-vous* (Francis Laï, René Rouzaud)

—?   *Les amants du dimanche* (composer/lyricist unknown) TR

1963

18 February   *Les gens* (Michelle Vendôme, Francis Laï)

Monsieur incognito (Florence Véran, Robert Gall)

Traqué (Florence Véran, Robert Gall)

21 February   *C'était pas moi* (Robert Gall, Francis Laï)

Le chant d'amour (Edith Piaf, Charles Dumont)

J'en ai tant bu (Michel Emer)

Margot Cœur-Gros (Michelle Vendôme, Florence Véran)

Tiens v'la un marin (Julien Bouquet, B Labadie)

All the above songs were recorded live at the Bobino Music Hall, Paris.

7 April   *L'homme de Berlin* (Michelle Vendome, Francis Laï) TR

The following songs, without known dates, are thought to exist on tape or acetate:

Black Boy; *Blues de février; Blues d'octobre; Clair de lune; Le gilet; Le pauvre homme; Le routier; Les pas; Moi je sais qu'on se reverra; Monsieur Lèvy; Pas une minute de plus; Poker* (Charles Aznavour, Pierre Roche); *Pourquoi m'as-tu trahi?; Sans faire de phrase; Un air d'accordéon* (Michel Emer); *Vol de nuit; Y avait une voix qui se lamentait; Le diable est près de moi* (Edith Piaf, Marguerite Monnot), *Mon amour je t'aime.*

Filmography

LA GARÇONNE   1936

    Script: Albert Dieaudonne
    Director: Jean de Limur
    Song: *Quand-même*
    Cast: Marie Bell, Arletty, Henri Rollan, Jean Worms, Jacques Catelain, Maurice Escande, La Môme Piaf.

MONTMARTRE-SUR-SEINE   1941

    Script: Georges Lacombe, Andre Cayette-Serge Veber
    Director: Georges Lacombe
    Songs: *L'Homme des bars, Tu es partout, Un coin tout bleu, j'ai dansé avec l'amour*
    Cast: Edith Piaf, Jean-Louis Barrault, Roger Duchesne, Paul Meurisse, Sylvie, Henri Vidal, Denise Grey, Huguette Faget.

ÉTOILE SANS LUMIERE   1946

    Script: Marcel Blistène
    Director: Marcel Blistène
    Band: Jacques Hélian
    Songs: *C'était une histoire d'amour, Adieu mon cœur, C'est merveilleux, Mariage, Le chant du pirate.*
    Cast: Edith Piaf, Mila Parely, Marcel Herrand, Yves Montand, Colette Brosset, Jules Berry, Serge Reggiani, Georges Vitray, Mady Berry.

LA BOÎTE À MUSIQUE {The Music Box}   1946

    Script: Walt Disney
    Song: *Les deux chapeaux* (Alice Blue Bonnet)
    Voices: Edith Piaf, Nelson Eddy, André Dassary

NEUF GARÇONS ET UN CŒUR   **1947**

    Script: Georges Freedland
  Director: Georges Freedland
   Songs: *La vie en rose, Les trois cloches, Sophie, Un refrain
             courait dans la rue, C'est pour ça.*
     Cast: Edith Piaf, Les Compagnons de la Chanson, Lyska
             Wells, Lucien Baroux, Marcel Vallée.

PARIS CHANTE TOUJOURS!   **1951**

    Script: Jacques Chabannes, R Feral
  Director: Pierre Montazel
     Band: Raymond Legrand
     Song: *L'hymne à l'amour*
     Cast: Raymond Souplex, Lucien Baroux, André
             Dassary, Georges Ulmer, Line Renaud, Tino Rossi,
             Edith Piaf, Yves Montand, Luis Mariano, Jean
             Sablon, Les Compagnons de la Chanson.

SI VERSAILLES M'ÉTAIT CONTE   **1953**

  Director: Sacha Guitry
    Music: Jean Francaix
     Song: *Le 'Ça Ira'*
     Cast: Jean Louis Barrault, Pauline Carton, Tino Rossi,
             Edith Piaf, Jean Marais, Gerard Philippe,
             Claudette Colbert, Orson Welles.

        The film was given a gala première in
        December 1953 at the Paris Opéra, when detachments
        of the *Garde Republicaine* lined the ceremonial
        stairway within the building. The proceeds from
        the film were donated to the Versailles
        reconstruction fund, and the film broke all
        records for box-office receipts.

FRENCH CAN-CAN   **1954**

  Director: Jean Renoir
    Script: André-Paul Antoine
    Music: Georges van Parys
     Song: *Sérénade du pavé*

Cast: Philippe Clay, Jean Gabin, Francoise Arnoul,
Patachou, Edith Piaf, Maria Felix, Jean-Roger
Caussimon.

BOUM SUR PARIS! 1954

Director: Maurice de Canonge
Songs: *Pour qu'elle soit jolie ma chanson, Je t'ai dans
la peau.*
Cast: Edith Piaf, Mouloudji, Juliette Greco, Tino Rossi.

LES AMANTS DE DEMAIN 1958

Director: Marcel Blistène
Script: Pierre Brasseur
Songs: *Les neiges de Finlande, Les amants de demain,
Fais comme si, Tant qu'il y aura des jours.*
Cast: Edith Piaf, Michel Auclair, Armand Mestral,
Mona Goya, Catherine Jan, Raymond Souplex,
Francis Blanche.

Theatre Productions

LE BEL INDIFFÉRENT   **1940**

Théâtre des Bouffes Parisiens
followed by tour.

Script: Jean Cocteau
Cast: Edith Piaf; Paul Meurisse (later replaced by
Jean Marconi).

LA P'TITE LILI   **1951**

ABC Music Hall

Script: Marcel Achard
Producer: Raymond Rouleau
Set: Lina de Nobili
Songs: *Demain il fera jour, L'homme que j'aimerais,*
Avant l'heure, Si si si, Petite si jolie, Du matin
Jusqu'au soir, Rien de rien, C'est toi.
Cast: Edith Piaf (Lili); Eddie Constantine (Spenser);
Robert Lamoureux (Mario); Howard Vernon (Eric);
Nora Coste (Martine); Katherine Kath (Irene);
Edith Fontaine (Henriette); supported by
Huguette Faget, Marcelle Praince,
Jeanne Silvestre, Joelle Robin, Robert Dalban,
Bugette, Henri Polage, Edith Jablan, Ketty
Albertini, Micheline Cevennes, Marie-Genevieve
Parmentier, Annie Duck, Maurice Nasil, Dangelys,
Robert Rollis, Germond, Gerard Kerise.

LE BEL INDIFFÉRENT   **1953**

Théâtre Marigny

Script: Jean Cocteau
Cast: Edith Piaf; Jacques Pills
Song: *Je t'ai dans la peau*

Film Tributes

1974

Director: Guy Casaril
Script: Based on the biography by Simone Berteaut
Cast: Brigitte Ariel, Pascale Christophe, Pierre Vernier, Jacques Duby, Guy Trejan
Songs: Interpreted by Edith Piaf and Betty Mars, include *L'accordéoniste* and *Le fanion de la Légion*.
It is interesting to note that the actress who played Piaf was selected by computer. The English language version of the film was called *Sparrow of Pigalle*, whereas the video, released in 1983, was called *Piaf, the Early Years*.

EDITH ET MARCEL   **1983**

Director: Claude Lelouch
Cast: Evelyne Bouix, Marcel Cerdan Jnr, Jacques Villeret, Francis Huster, Charles Aznavour, Jean-Claude Brialy, Charlotte de Turckheim.
Songs: *L'effet que tu me fais, Et moi, Le diable de la Bastille, Hymne a l'amour, Les mots d'amour, Je t'ai dans la peau, Le chant d'amour, C'est de la faut à tes yeux, Mon Dieu, Comme moi, C'est peut-être ça, Bal dans ma rue, C'est merveilleux, La vie en rose, L'homme que j'aimerais, Un homme comme les autres, Margot cœur-gros, La foule.* (Interpreted by Piaf). *C'est un gars, Je n'attendais que toi, Le fanion de la légion, La prière, Viens pleurer au creux de mon épaule, Avant toi.* (Interpreted by Charles Aznavour and Mama Bea, who also sang *L'Effet que tu me fais*).

In 1968 Trianon Films produced a short, but excellent biography, *Edith Piaf*, in black and white and narrated by Alan Badel. Piaf was seen singing *La foule* at the Paris Olympia in 1962, and other songs complementing newsreel reports were *Mon légionnaire, Entre Saint Ouen et Clignancourt*, and *Milord*. This film is important in that it shows Belleville in the early thirties.

Revues

Producer:	Libby Morris
Music:	New Arrangements by Chuck Mallett and Frank Stafford
Lyrics:	Additional English lyrics by Fran Landesman, Ronnie Bridges and Peter Reeves.
Cast:	Libby Morris, Peter Reeves, Maureen Scott, Clifton Todd.
Songs:	Under the Paris Skies (*Sous le ciel de Paris*)

Little Sparrow of Paris (*Toujours aimer*)
My Friend John (*La Goualante du pauvre Jean*)
Milord
The Accordionist (*L'accordéoniste*)
In Amsterdam (*C'est à Hambourg*)
Lovers in Paris (*Les amants de Paris*)
It's Lovely Loving You (*Il fait bon t'aimer*)
If You Love Me, Really Love Me (*Hymne a l'amour*)
Padam padam
I Don't Care (*Je m'en fous pas mal*)
Gypsy Boy (*Le gitan et la fille*)
Song of Catherine (*La chanson de Catherine*)
Poor Lost Louise (*Margot Cœur-Gros*)
Les flons-flons du bal
Bravo for the Clown (*Bravo pour le clown*)
My Lost Melody
Love is Like Champagne (*Mon manège à moi*)
I Hope (*Faut pas qu'il se figure*)
An Exceptional Spring (*Il y avait*)
Strange Town (*La ville inconnue*)
Beside My Legionnaire (*Mon légionnaire*)
The Crowd (*La foule*)
The Devil Who Danced (*Le diable de la Bastille*)
La vie en rose
In a World of Our Own (*Les gens*)
The Right to Love (*Le droit d'aimer*)
La vie, l'amour
Two People Kiss (*Dans leur baiser*)

181

The Lovers (*Les amants*)
Please God (*Mon Dieu*)
In the Waiting Room (*Salle d'attente*)
Hands (*Les mains*)
The White Shirts (*Les blouses blanches*)
Cri du cœur
The Way Love Goes (*A quoi ça sert l'amour*)
Non je ne regrette rien

EDITH PIAF, PARMI NOUS   **1983**
                                                       Bobino Theatre, Paris

An intimate, audio-visual revue, introduced by Piaf's recorded voice, and featuring her most celebrated songs performed by Betty Mars and Jack Mells, accompanied by the Jean Sala Trio.

Songs performed by Betty Mars: *Tu es née à Belleville, Comme un moineau, Les mots d'amour, Mon manège à moi, L'homme à la moto, Milord, Non je ne regrette rien.*

Songs performed by Jack Mels: *Je m'imagine, Je n'en connais pas la fin, Marie la Française, Retour, Avec ce soleil, Bravo pour le clown, Eden Blues, Mon Dieu.*

Songs performed en duo: *Moi je sais qu'on se reverra, A quoi ça sert l'amour, Roulez tambours, Hymne a l'amour, Les trois cloches, C'est peut-etre ça, Bout de femme, Légende (with Piaf)*

Theatre Tributes

PIAF   by Pam Gems

This astonishing masterpiece – astonishing in that although it is based on
Simone Berteaut's biography, and presents Piaf as she really was, warts
and all, it still manages to convince us of her deep love and understanding
of the human condition – opened in 1979 in a provincial theatre. It was
an immediate hit, and progressed via the West End to New York, since
which time it has toured Britain to packed houses. The original production
had characterisations of Josephine Baker and Marlene Dietrich; the latter
was removed in 1982 when Marlene objected to anyone playing her whilst
she was still alive. Subsequent 'Piafs' have included Helen Cotterill and
Yvonne Edgell. The original London production, which opened on 5
October 1978 at The Other Place, Stratford-upon-Avon, was directed by
Howard Davies and designed by Douglas Heap, with the following cast:
Jane Lapotaire (Piaf)
Zoë Wanamaker (Toine)
Carmen du Sautoy (Madeleine)
Darlene Johnson (Marlene)
Susanna Bishop (Nurse)
Conrad Asquith (Inspector, Georges, Barman)
Bill Buffery (Louis, Butcher, Lucien, Dope pusher)
Ian Charleson (Man at rehearsal, Pierre)
Geoffrey Freshwater (Manager)
James Griffiths (Leplée, Jean)
Allan Hendrick (Emil, Jacko, Eddie)
Anthony Higgins (German soldier, Angelo)
Ian Reddington (Paul, American sailor, Physiotherapist)
Malcom Storry (Legionnaire, Jacques, German soldier, Marcel, Ameri-
can sailor, Théo)

Television Biographies

I REGRET NOTHING
1970
BBC Television, 75 mins

Producer: Michael Houldey
Narrator: David de Keyser
With Edith Piaf, Charles Aznavour, Eddie Constantine, Jacques Pills, Simone Margantin, Michel Emer, Yves Montand, Les Compagnons de la Chanson, Marcel Blistène, Théo Sarapo.
Songs: *Non je ne regrette rien, Je sais comment, Si si si, Les mômes de la cloche, Entre St Ouen et Clignancourt, Mon légionnaire, C'est merveilleux, Les trois cloches, Bravo pour le clown, L'accordéoniste, N'y vas pas Manuel, Télégramme, Enfin le printemps, Une enfant, La vie en rose, La Goualante du pauvre Jean, Je t'ai dans la peau, Les gens, Heureuse, La foule, L'homme à la moto, Le droit d'aimer, Milord, A quoi ça sert l'amour, Hymne à l'amour, C'est à Hambourg, Mon manège à moi*, No Regrets.

ALL YOU NEED IS LOVE
1973
Independent Television

The section devoted to Piaf included her performing *Milord, A quoi ça sert l'amour, La vie en rose, Hymne à L'amour*, and *Non je ne regrette rien*.

PIAF (ARENA)
1979
BBC Television, 20 mins

Featuring Jane Lapotaire, promoting her role in Pam Gems' play *Piaf*, the programme included rare film footage of Piaf, and recorded scenes from the play.
Songs: *La vie en rose, Les mots d'amour, L'accordéoniste, A quoi ça sert l'amour, Le droit d'aimer* and *Les mômes de la cloche*.

British Radio Biographies

PIAF THE ENTERTAINER   1973

Producer: Stanley Willamson
Narrator: Geoffrey Wheeler
Miriam Karlin narrated passages from *Ma Vie*, and the programme included extracts of interviews from *I Regret Nothing*.
Songs: *Non je ne regrette rien, Milord, Mon légionnaire, L'accordéoniste, No Regrets, La vie en rose*, Hymn to Love, *Je t'ai dans la peau, Bravo pour le clown, Mon Dieu, A quoi ça sert l'amour.*

PORTRAIT OF PIAF   1974

Producer: Lawrence Bedford
Script: Thomas Thompson
Presenter: Elizabeth Welch

This fascinating three-part programme featured more than one hundred famous Piaf songs, and some rare ones, including the Radio-Cité broadcast in 1936 of *Le fanion de la Légion*. There were extracts of interviews from *I Regret Nothing* with additional tributes from Juliette Greco, Nana Mouskouri, and Jacques Canetti. Passages from her autobiographies were read by Nicolette Bernard, and the theme for each programme was 'My Lost Melody'. Miss Welch was responsible for introducing *La vie en rose* to British audiences during the late forties, and at the time of writing still includes it in her act.

EDITH PIAF   1981

This programme was broadcast by BBC Radio Leeds to coincide with the Leeds Playhouse production of Pam Gems' play. It included several of the songs featured in the play, and an interview with the star, Helen Cotterill.

TROUBADOURS OF FRENCH SONG   1983

Presented by the French actor-broadcaster Daniel Pageon, this represented a somewhat sketchy and inaccurate account of the singer's life, and featured six of her most celebrated songs. The theme song for this and Pageon's other series *Nights at the Paris Olympia* was Charles Trenet's

Moi, J'Aime le Music-Hall, itself used for France Inter's enormously successful series *Les cingles du Music-Hall*, presented by Jean-Christophe Averty and often featuring rare records and tapes of Piaf, Damia, and Marie Dubas.

Recordings:

Ninety-five per-cent of the Piaf output has been released in France between 1936 and the present day. Most of her songs have been released in Britain at some time or other, and her actual records are too numerous to mention. Worldwide, her most sought-after records have been the extended-play and ten-inch LPs released by Pathé-Marconi between 1953 and 1968. All have been deleted, and are as follows:

Extended Play

ESRF 1022:   *La Goualante du pauvre Jean; Heureuse; Soeur Anne; Johnny tu n'es pas un ange.*

ESRF 1023:   *Padam padam; Jézèbel; Mariage; Les amants de Venise.*

ESRF 1036:   *C'est à Hambourg; Le chemin des forains; L'homme au piano; Retour.*

ESRF 1051:   *La vie en rose; Les trois cloches; Hymne à l'amour; L'accordéoniste.*

ESRF 1070:   *Les amants d'un jour; Soudain une vallée; L'homme à la moto; Avant nous.*

ESRF 1135:   *Les grognards; Les prisons du roi.*

ESRF 1136:   *La foule; Comme moi; Salle d'attente.*

ESRF 1174:   *Mon manège à moi; Fais comme si; Le ballet des cœurs; Un étranger.*

ESRF 1197:   *Edith Piaf chante Jo Moustaki: Eden Blues; Les orgues de Barbarie; Le gitan et la fille.* The sleeve notes were written by Georges Brassens.

ESRF 1198:   *Edith Piaf chante les airs du film 'Les amants de demain': Les amants de demain; Les neiges de Finlande; Fais comme si; Tant qu'il y aura des jours.* Sleeve notes were written by Marcel Blistène.

ESRF 1215:   *C'est un homme terrible; Tatave; Je me souviens d'une chanson.*

ESRF 1245:   *Milord; Je sais comment.*

ESRF 1262:   *Boulevard du crime; La ville inconnue; La vie L'amour.*

ESRF 1289:   *Les amants merveilleux; C'est l'amour; Cri du cœur.*

ESRF 1292:   *Ouragan; Opinion publique; Le vieux piano.*

ESRF 1305:   *Edith Piaf chante Charles Dumont: Mon Dieu; Les flons-flons du bal; La belle histoire d'amour.* Sleeve notes written by Piaf.

ESRF 1306:   *Exodus; Marie Trottoir; Dans leur baiser.*

ESRF 1312:   *Non je ne regrette rien; Les mots d'amour; Toujours aimer; Mon vieux Lucien.*

ESRF 1319:   *Edith Piaf et Charles Dumont chantent L'amour: C'est peut-être ça* (sung by Piaf); *La fille qui pleurait dans la rue* (sung by Dumont); *Les amants* (sung by Piaf and Dumont).*

ESRF 1357:   *Chansons à la une: Toi tu l'entends pas; Ça fait drôle; fallait-il; Polichinelle.*

ESRF 1361:   *Emporte-moi; Le petit brouillard; Musique à tout va; A quoi ça sert l'amour?*

ESRF 1373:   *Le droit d'aimer; Le rendez-vous; Roulez tambours.*

ESRF 1466:   *Edith Piaf avec les Compagnons de la Chanson: Les trois cloches; Dans les prisons de Nantes; Le roi a fait battre tambour; Céline.*

ESRF 1921:   *L'homme de Berlin; Traque; Le diable de la Bastille; Les gens.* Sleeve notes written by Francis Laï.

Long Play

FS 1008:   *La vie en rose; C'est de la faut a tes yeux; La fête continue; Hymne à l'amour; Je hais les dimanches; Padam padam; Plus bleu que tes yeux; Jezebel.*

FS 1037:   *Soeur Anne; Heureuse; N'y va pas Manuel; Et moi; Les amants de Venise; La goualante du pauvre Jean; Johnny tu n'es pas un ange; Le 'ça ira'; Bravo pour le clown; L'effet que tu me fais.*

FS 1049:   *Edith Piaf a l'Olympia: Heureuse; Avec ce soleil; C'est à Hambourg; Légende; Enfin le printemps; Miséricorde; Je t'ai dans la peau; La goualante du pauvre Jean; Bravo pour le clown; Padam padam.*

ES 1083:   *Huit chansons nouvelles: C'est l'amour; Ouragan; T'es beau tu sais; Cri du cœur; Le vieux piano; Les amants merveilleux; Je suis a toi; Opinion publique.*

ES 1103:   *Le billard Électrique; Faut-pas qu'il se figure;* Carmen's Story; *Qu'il était triste cet Anglais.*

FS 1104:   *Les amants de teruel; Quatorze Juillet; Toi tu l'entends pas; Polichinelle; Ça fait drôle; On cherche un Auguste; Une valse; Fallait-il.*

Songs written for Théo Sarapo by Edith Piaf

1962–1970 Pathé-Marconi

1962
Chez Sabine

Les mains

1963
Les enfants de la mode
Un dimanche à Londres
La bande en noir
Defense de . . .

1964
Bluff!
Chanson d'amour d'aujourd'hui